DRAMA CLASSICS

The Drama Classics series aims to offer the world's greatest plays in affordable paperback editions for students, actors and theatregoers. The hallmarks of the series are accessible introductions, uncluttered texts and an overall theatrical perspective.

Given that readers may be encountering a particular play for the first time, the introduction seeks to fill in the theatrical/historical background and to outline the chief themes rather than concentrate on interpretational and textual analysis. Similarly the play-texts themselves are free of footnotes and other interpolations: instead there is an end-glossary of 'difficult' words and phrases.

The texts of the English-language plays in the series have been prepared taking full account of all existing scholarship. The foreign-language plays have been newly translated into a modern English that is both actable and accurate: many of the translators regularly have their work staged professionally.

Edited until his early death by Kenneth McLeish, the Drama Classics series continues with his aim of providing a first-class library of dramatic literature representing the best of world theatre.

Associate editors:
Professor Trevor R. Griffiths
Visiting Professor in Humanities, Universities of Exeter and Hertfordshire
Dr Colin Counsell
School of Humanities, Arts and Languages, London Metropolitan University

DRAMA CLASSICS   *the first hundred*

The publishers welcome
suggestions for further titles

DRAMA CLASSICS

IVANOV
by
Anton Chekhov

translated and introduced by
Stephen Mulrine

NICK HERN BOOKS
London
www.nickhernbooks.co.uk

A Drama Classic

Ivanov first published in Great Britain in this translation
as a paperback original in 2010 by Nick Hern Books Limited,
14 Larden Road, London W3 7ST

Copyright in the introduction © 2010 Nick Hern Books Ltd
Copyright in this translation © 2010 Stephen Mulrine

Stephen Mulrine has asserted his right to be identified as the
translator of this work

Typeset by Country Setting, Kingsdown, Kent CT14 8ES
Printed and bound in Great Britain by CPI Bookmarque, Croydon, Surrey

A CIP catalogue record for this book is available from the British Library

ISBN 978 1 84842 068 7

Introduction

Anton Chekhov (1860–1904)

Anton Pavlovich Chekhov was born in Taganrog, a seaport in South Russia, in 1860. By his own account, his childhood was far from idyllic. His father Pavel was a domestic tyrant, fanatically religious, and Chekhov and his brothers were forced to rise before dawn to sing in the local church choir, then work long hours after school, in his family's grocer's shop.

Taganrog was in decline, but its Greek shipping community was relatively wealthy, and Chekhov was first sent to a Greek-language school, which his father naively regarded as the highway to a lucrative career. After a wasted year, Chekhov was enrolled in the local high school, where he stayed, an unremarkable scholar, until 1879.

His last years at the Taganrog school were spent apart from his family, however, since his bankrupt father had fled to Moscow, where Chekhov's elder brothers were already students. Chekhov completed his studies, entered Moscow University's Faculty of Medicine, and at the age of nineteen became the family's principal breadwinner, writing short comic pieces to supplement his student allowance.

By the time he qualified in 1884, Chekhov's literary ambitions were already in conflict with what he regarded as his true vocation. Indeed, until his own health collapsed, he continued to practise medicine, mostly as an unpaid service to nearby rural communities. Chekhov was almost certainly infected with tuberculosis from childhood, and the disease was in its terminal stages before he would permit an independent diagnosis. In addition to frequent haemorrhaging from the lungs, which forced him to spend the winters in the warm South, Chekhov also suffered from a variety of other chronic ailments, yet his work rate was little short of heroic. In 1899, when he agreed to sell the rights in his works to the publisher Marks, they already filled ten volumes, and the critical consensus is that his short stories are an unparalleled achievement, with the four great plays of his mature dramatic method, *The Seagull*, *Uncle Vanya*, *Three Sisters* and *The Cherry Orchard*, no less important.

Human relationships are the substance of all Chekhov's work, and it is perhaps no surprise that this most intimate of writers remained elusive in his own. Although fond of women, and pursued by several, Chekhov characteristically retreated as they advanced, and it is a reasonable assumption that the happiness of his brief married life, with the actress Olga Knipper, depended to an extent on the lengthy periods of separation forced on the couple by the dramatist's poor health, and Olga's busy metropolitan career.

Finally, in a despairing effort to postpone the inevitable, Chekhov travelled with Olga to Germany for medical treatment. In July 1904, following a heart attack, he died in the spa town of Badenweiler, at the age of forty-four.

Ivanov: **What Happens in the Play**

At the beginning of Act One, Nikolai Ivanov, a middle-aged provincial landowner, is sitting in his garden reading, when Borkin, his estate manager, returns drunk from a shooting party and, by way of a jest, points his rifle at him. Ivanov is far from amused, and even less so when Borkin reminds him that the estate workers are due to be paid next day, and there is no money for them. Ivanov's wife, Anna Petrovna, meanwhile, is confined indoors owing to ill health, with Ivanov's uncle, Count Shabelsky, keeping her company.

Anna Petrovna, formerly Sarra Abramson, comes from a wealthy Jewish family, who disowned her when she gave up her religion to marry Ivanov, so with no dowry to draw on and a failing estate, Ivanov is virtually bankrupt, furthermore heavily in debt to the chairman of the local rural council, Lebedev. Borkin is frustrated at what he sees as Ivanov's incompetence, but his advice on how to repair the estate's fortunes amounts to thinly disguised extortion, and Ivanov shows no interest in them, pinning his hopes rather on persuading Lebedev to extend his loan.

Dr Lvov, the physician attending Anna Petrovna, urges Ivanov to take her to the Crimea – she has tuberculosis, he says, and a sojourn in the warm South is essential for her health. Ivanov can't afford it, he tells the doctor, but later, when they are alone, Lvov accuses him of actively damaging his wife's chances of recovery by neglect. Ivanov admits his guilt, and recounts the sacrifices his wife made in marrying him, but claims to be powerless to change his ways. After they go out, Anna Petrovna and Shabelsky emerge from the house. The Count, like his nephew, strapped for cash, reveals a dark vein of cynicism under his bantering manner.

Anna Petrovna goes indoors, and Shabelsky is joined by Dr Lvov and Ivanov, still debating the issue of Ivanov's callous behaviour towards his wife. Ivanov announces his intention to go out that evening over to the Lebedevs' on business, but Dr Lvov is convinced his motives are much less transparent, and suspects Ivanov's real interest lies in the Lebedevs' young daughter, Sasha. When Ivanov comes out of the house, dressed for visiting, Shabelsky begs leave to accompany him, and Ivanov reluctantly agrees. Anna Petrovna implores him to stay with her, but the truth of the matter is that he no longer loves her, and determines to go, despite a deeply troubled conscience. Left alone, Anna Petrovna and Lvov reflect gloomily on her situation. Lvov makes it plain he regards Ivanov as a hypocritical scoundrel, and cannot understand why she continues to endure such cruelty. Anna Petrovna angrily defends her husband – Lvov is young, and unmarried, he has no insight into human nature, and no right to judge people. Despite her illness, Anna Petrovna orders a carriage to take her to the Lebedev house in pursuit of her husband.

The Lebedevs' drawing room that same evening is the setting for Act Two; Pavel Lebedev and his wife Zinaida are celebrating their daughter's birthday, and several guests are present, some playing cards, others drifting in and out from the garden. The action begins with Zinaida greeting Mrs Babakin, a wealthy young widow; other guests include Avdotya, an elderly woman friend, and Kosykh, an excise official. They are eventually joined by Lebedev and Sasha, and the conversation inevitably comes round to marriage and the scarcity of eligible young men. Lebedev expresses some admiration for Ivanov, unfortunately already married, but Zinaida doesn't share his view, and a heated argument develops between Zinaida and her daughter on the subject of Ivanov's character and his foolhardy decision to marry a Jewess. Other guests contribute more gossip about Ivanov and his devious estate manager, until Sasha can bear it no longer and harangues them for their mental laziness.

Ivanov and Shabelsky arrive at this juncture, and while Ivanov remains silent, the Count flirts with Mrs Babakin and entertains the company with his outrageous opinions. The conversation then turns to Dr Lvov, and both Shabelsky and Sasha voice their distrust of his ostentatious 'honest man' pose. Borkin, Ivanov's steward, is next to arrive, in a decidedly party mood, and his proposal to set off fireworks in the garden is enthusiastically welcomed.

Left alone with Sasha, Ivanov pours out his heart to her, admitting to a permanent state of depression and hopelessness. Sasha is deeply touched and, half-joking, suggests they should run away together. They are then briefly interrupted by Zinaida, and Ivanov takes the opportunity to ask her for an extension to his loan, which the notoriously frugal and grasping Zinaida predictably refuses. Finally, Anna Petrovna arrives, escorted by Dr Lvov, continuing their disagreement from earlier in the evening, with Anna Petrovna still doggedly defending her husband's character. As they go out of the drawing room, Mrs Babakin enters, pursued by Borkin and Shabelsky. Borkin first asks Mrs Babakin to lend him some money, and then brazenly offers the Count to her as a marriage partner – her wealth in exchange for the title of Countess.

When Ivanov and Sasha re-enter from the garden, it is
plain that Sasha has declared her love for him. Ivanov is
overwhelmed, scarcely daring to believe that he might
embark on a new life with her. They seal their mutual joy
with a kiss, just as Anna Petrovna walks into the room.

Act Three takes place some weeks later in Ivanov's study,
where Shabelsky, Borkin and Lebedev are engaged in
desultory conversation, fuelled by snacks and vodka, while
they wait for Ivanov. Borkin returns to his theme of
marriage, urging Shabelsky to make up his mind about the
widow Babakin. Dr Lvov, who has been attending to the
now seriously ill Anna Petrovna, looks in to ask if Ivanov
has come home yet, but storms out in disgust at Shabelsky's
jocular manner. Kosykh is next to appear, but so obsessed is
he with the card game he has just lost that Shabelsky
threatens to shoot him. As Kosykh runs out, he collides
with Avdotya on her way in, but the arrival of Ivanov,
quickly followed by Dr Lvov, puts an end to the merriment.
Lebedev wants a word with Ivanov in private; it is about
money, of course – Zinaida is demanding that Ivanov pay
the interest on his loan, without further delay. Lebedev is
genuinely embarrassed by the situation, and when Ivanov
confesses his inability to pay, Lebedev offers to give him the
money himself, from a secret hoard, unknown to Zinaida.
Ivanov, however, seems beyond help. Lebedev's well-
intentioned efforts to bolster Ivanov's spirits, naively
including an invitation to visit Sasha, come to nothing.

After Lebedev leaves, Ivanov embarks on a lengthy
soliloquy, reviewing the events of his wasted life – his
ruined estate, his ill-starred marriage, his moral paralysis –
compounded by shame and guilt, at his callous treatment of

his dying wife. Ivanov, mentally and physically exhausted, even contemplates suicide.

At this point, Dr Lvov returns and immediately launches into a sustained verbal assault on Ivanov, accusing him of having married Anna Petrovna solely for her dowry, and when that was not forthcoming, of having turned his attentions to the Lebedevs' daughter for the sake of *her* dowry. Ivanov's response is not to deny his guilt, but to challenge Dr Lvov's false reading of his character. Fully conscious of his own shortcomings, Ivanov nonetheless rejects the portrait Dr Lvov paints of him, as a cynical, calculating sociopath. The encounter ends in bitter recrimination and mutual misunderstanding, but not before Sasha makes an unexpected entrance – confirming the doctor's worst suspicions about her relationship with Ivanov.

In fact, Ivanov has not seen Sasha for some weeks, and she has come to reproach him. Ivanov's black mood is not easily dispelled, and he fears for the effect Sasha's visit might have on his wife. Sasha tries to convince him that he can't be held responsible for his emotions and, to every protestation of worthlessness he makes, she responds with unconditional love – what she describes as 'active' love, the more intensely felt, *because* it is undertaken as a rescue attempt. Sasha is determined to redeem Ivanov by the power of love, but for the present she urges him to stay with Anna Petrovna, and cherish her. At this moment, Borkin's breezy entrance shatters the mood, and Ivanov flies into a rage and chases him out.

Finally, Anna Petrovna appears. She has discovered that Sasha has been with her husband, and bluntly accuses him of betraying her. She further insists that he married her only for her money. Ivanov furiously denies the charge, but eventually his patience snaps, and he does the unforgivable – tells her to her face of Dr Lvov's diagnosis, and the certainty of her impending death.

Between Acts Three and Four a year has elapsed, during which Anna Petrovna has indeed died. Preparations are under way, in the Lebedevs' house, for the wedding of their daughter Sasha and Ivanov. Dr Lvov enters, newly arrived and vowing to put an end to the charade by publicly denouncing Ivanov as a calculating scoundrel. Guests drift in and out of the sitting room, the inveterate card players are still complaining, the widow Babakin still has her eye on Shabelsky's title, Shabelsky still hasn't made up his mind. Lebedev, again doing Zinaida's bidding, draws Sasha aside for a private conversation. More than a little embarrassed, he tells his daughter that Zinaida has agreed to settle a dowry on her, but is insisting that Ivanov's debt will be deducted from it. Sasha indignantly dismisses all thought of a dowry, and a bewildered Lebedev is forced reluctantly to admit his own reservations about the marriage, in particular the difference in their ages.

Sasha then confesses that she is deeply unhappy – Ivanov seems constantly depressed, and evasive, but when Lebedev urges her to give him up, she reaffirms her commitment to save Ivanov from himself, by the power of love. At this point, they are interrupted by Shabelsky, seeking to borrow money from Lebedev, and Mrs Babakin, in pursuit of Shabelsky, who finally dashes her hopes of becoming a countess, reducing her to tears. Zinaida then adds her piece to the collective misery, before Ivanov, defying wedding etiquette, arrives unexpectedly to speak in private with Sasha.

Alone finally, Ivanov implores Sasha to call the wedding off – he is an old man, no fit husband for her, and burdened with terrible guilt besides. Sasha tries to stem the flow of Ivanov's tirade of self-loathing and despair, even enlisting her father's help, but Ivanov is not to be persuaded. No matter what Lebedev says – he even offers to ignore Zinaida's wishes, and gift the couple a large sum of money – Ivanov remains adamant: there will be no wedding.

Meanwhile, the guests are already assembling at the church, and the best man has come to escort the groom to the ceremony. Dr Lvov then appears and formally denounces Ivanov in front of the whole company. Sasha answers him in kind, pouring scorn on his self-righteous posturing. At the last moment, her defiant stance seems to have renewed Ivanov's courage, but instead of leaving along with her, Ivanov suddenly produces a revolver and shoots himself.

Chekhov the Dramatist

Chekhov might be described as the writer's writer, not only on account of his work, and the fund of wisdom in his correspondence, but also because he presents a model of the tireless self-improver, grinding his way from penny-a-line squibs in the comic papers to the status of modern classic in both his preferred genres – and all in the space of a mere two decades.

In that respect, the year 1887–88 represents a turning-point in his career, with the staging of his first four-act play, *Ivanov* (leaving aside the unplayable epic now known as *Platonov*), and the publication of his short story *The Steppe* in one of the prestige 'thick journals', 'The Northern Herald'. The same year also saw his official recognition as a major Russian writer with the award of the Pushkin Prize, by the Academy of Sciences. Chekhov had arrived, it seems, though the reception given to *Ivanov*, premiered in Moscow to mixed cheering and booing, suggested he had done so some way ahead of his audience.

That is broadly the story of Chekhov's whole dramatic career, and it is significant that the main bone of contention in *Ivanov*, dividing first-nighters into partisans and scoffers, was the author's seeming abdication of any clear moral stance. After some changes, however, the play was successfully revived in St Petersburg, and Chekhov was emboldened to offer his next play, *The Wood Demon*, for production in Moscow the following year. Alas, *The Wood Demon* was a flop, and in the light of Chekhov's developing method, it is interesting to note that criticism generally centred on its lack of action, and dreary slice-of-life dialogue. Chekhov withdrew the play in disgust, and buried it deep within his mysterious creative processes, whence it emerged in 1897, in the radically altered form of *Uncle Vanya*, one of the greatest works of the modern theatre.

Between times, Chekhov endured the catastrophic failure of *The Seagull*, an experience which encapsulated everything that was wrong with the Russian theatre of his day, and that his work did so much to change. *The Seagull* was premiered in October 1896 at the Alexandrinsky Theatre in St Petersburg, which in Chekhov's day was both the administrative and cultural capital of the country, and it was especially important that his new venture should succeed there. Unfortunately, the play spent almost a year in the hands of the censors, which meant that the actors received their scripts a bare week before opening night. Worse still, *The Seagull* had been commissioned from Chekhov as a vehicle for the benefit performance of one of the Alexandrinsky's stars, Levkeeva, a mature comedienne with a large and vociferous following. She had originally been billed to play Arkadina, but had decided instead to appear in a three-act comedy, ironically titled *This Happy Day*, to be staged immediately after *The Seagull*. The disappointment of her fans, made to endure four acts of Chekhov, is not difficult to imagine, and the play was greeted with whistling and jeering almost from its opening lines.

After the fiasco of *The Seagull*, Chekhov fled from St Petersburg, and although the play's fortunes improved with 'normal' audiences, the generally hostile reviews made him resolve to quit the theatre for ever. Fortunately, *Uncle Vanya* appears to have been already on the stocks, and while the course of its development out of *The Wood Demon* remains unclear, it almost certainly followed the writing of *The Seagull*. At any rate, *Uncle Vanya* first surfaced in 1897, when Chekhov had it published.

The following year, 1898, saw the coming together of Chekhov and the newly founded Moscow Art Theatre – commonly presented as a marriage made in theatre heaven. Its founders, Stanislavsky and Nemirovich-Danchenko, shared Chekhov's dissatisfaction with the Russian theatre of the day, its bombastic acting, poor technical standards, and outmoded star system. Stanislavsky, a wealthy merchant's son, ran his own amateur theatre company, and Nemirovich-Danchenko lectured in drama at the Moscow Philharmonic School, where his students included the future director Vsevolod Meyerhold, and Olga Knipper, eventually to become Chekhov's wife.

The Moscow Art Theatre was the product of their determination to create a new kind of professional theatre, in which the ensemble, rather than the individual actor, would be paramount, and which would pay close attention not only to the text, but also to scenery, costumes, lighting, incidental music and sound effects – even the design of the programme and the colour of the curtain. There were to be no 'benefit' performances, and no stars; the repertoire, Nemirovich-Danchenko's responsibility, would be chosen on literary merit alone, and an actor might play the lead in one production, and carry a spear in the next; in Stanislavsky's famous dictum: 'There are no small parts, only small actors.' The new company also had a mission to educate audiences to a proper respect for the drama, and even excluded latecomers – unheard of in the commercial theatre of the day.

What Chekhov's plays needed – natural, unforced speaking, even-handed ensemble playing and lengthy, painstaking rehearsal – appeared to be exactly what the Moscow Art Theatre could bring to them, and indeed it can be argued that much of Stanislavsky's famous 'method' was developed precisely to accommodate Chekhov's writing. And if the relationship turned out to be less than wholly blissful, it is to their credit nonetheless that Chekhov continued to write for the stage, including the two masterpieces specially commissioned by the Moscow Art Theatre, *Three Sisters* and *The Cherry Orchard*.

The rapturous reception accorded to *The Seagull* at its Moscow premiere on 17 December 1898 has passed into legend. Its success not only restored Chekhov's confidence, it also rescued the fortunes of the Moscow Art Theatre, who were now eager to attempt *Uncle Vanya*, which had already been staged in the provinces. Unfortunately, Chekhov had promised the play to the Maly Theatre, but a number of script changes being demanded by its literary committee gave him a legitimate excuse for withdrawing the offer. *Uncle Vanya* was thus produced by the Moscow Art Theatre in October 1899 – in terms of its reception, more consolidation than triumph, but sufficiently encouraging to focus Chekhov's mind on a new subject – the lives of three sisters in a remote provincial town.

Three Sisters opened in January 1901, and while it was certainly no failure, neither it, nor *The Cherry Orchard* three years later, managed to repeat the smash hit of *The Seagull*. By the spring of 1903, when he began committing *The Cherry Orchard* to paper, Chekhov had little more than a year to live, and his health had deteriorated to such an extent that he could write only a few lines a day. Nonetheless, he was able to attend rehearsals at the Moscow Art Theatre in December, and *The Cherry Orchard* was premiered on Chekhov's forty-fourth birthday, 17 January 1904. Three months later, Chekhov was dead, and the brief span of his career as a dramatist complete. We can only guess at what he might have achieved, had he lived as long as Ibsen, or even Shakespeare, but in a mere handful of plays, Chekhov has given the classic repertoire not only a unique vision, but also, in his off-centre, low-key rhetoric, one of its most compelling modern voices.

Ivanov: A Work in Progress

Chekhov's career as a dramatist effectively begins with the Moscow production of *Ivanov* in November 1887, but his first serious venture in the medium took place six or seven years earlier, when he submitted a full-length play, now generally titled *Platonov* to the Maly Theatre in St Petersburg. *Platonov*, unearthed among Chekhov's papers long after his death, received its first performance in Stockholm only in 1954. Reasons for its rejection and subsequent neglect are not hard to find, and although its melodramatic content – suicide, murder, shooting, stabbing, poisoning – may not have been the primary objection, given the Russian theatre of the day, its notional playing time of six hours made it virtually unstageable. Slimmed down, however, *Platonov* has since been successfully revived on a number of occasions, and the critical consensus is that both in style and content, the unique character of Chekhov's mature drama, if not his economy of means, is already foreshadowed in this apprentice work.

Chekhov's response to the rejection of *Platonov* was to suppress his theatrical ambitions for several years, until a Moscow impresario, F. A. Korsh, commissioned him to write a new full-length play. Korsh's private theatre, which presented mainly farces, was one of a number of such enterprises prompted by the ending of the government monopoly on theatre in Moscow and St Petersburg in 1882. Clearly, Korsh would have expected 'Antosha Chekhonte' (the *nom de plume* under which he had written his early humorous sketches) to deliver a sure-fire comic hit, and

Korsh must have been surprised when, two weeks later, the four acts of *Ivanov* landed on his desk.

By his own lights, Korsh did his best with *Ivanov*, casting the noted actor V. N. Davydov in the title role – initially with Chekhov's wholehearted approval. However, after only four rehearsals, the first performance, on 19 November 1887, was alternately applauded and jeered by a bewildered audience, not helped by the fact that several actors had forgotten their lines, and ad-libbed throughout, as Chekhov had gloomily anticipated in a letter to his brother Alexander, in which he described the actors as 'capricious and arrogant, semi-literate poseurs who would sell their soul to the devil for a better part than their rivals'.

Chekhov had categorised *Ivanov* as a comedy, but of a sort unfamiliar to his audience. Though he was not averse to melodramatic effect, at any stage in his career, he was highly critical of his contemporaries, who 'stuffed their plays with angels, devils and buffoons' – stereotypes detached from reality. In *Ivanov*, he declared, there were no saints or sinners – nobody was to be accused, or justified, at least not by the author. While simpler souls took exception to the hero's death (from heart failure, in this version, brought on by Dr Lvov's public denunciation), more sophisticated critics puzzled over Chekhov's take on the literary type of the 'superfluous man', typified by Pushkin's Onegin, Lermontov's Pechorin, Turgenev's Rudin or Bazarov. How were they to judge Chekhov's self-obsessed melancholic? On his own terms? Ivanov scarcely bothers to defend himself against the worst Dr Lvov can throw at him, even to the charge of culpability for his wife's death. Ironically, the key to understanding Ivanov's behaviour is to accept that human beings are too complex to be understood – at least by such a facile interpreter as the self-righteous Dr Lvov.

In general, the open-and-shut case is anathema to Chekhov; Ivanov's treatment of Anna Petrovna merits condemnation by any standard, but the loudest voices raised against him, apart from his own, belong to Dr Lvov, a humourless pillar of rectitude, and a chorus of backbiting money-grubbers and vodka-swillers. By contrast, the most sympathetic characters, Lebedev, Sasha and Anna Petrovna think highly of him. Anna Petrovna, in spite of her devastating assault on Ivanov's character after she learns of Sasha's clandestine visit, angrily defends her husband, for the talented and hard-working man he once was, against Dr Lvov's contemptuous dismissal of him.

This core dilemma, which Chekhov's audiences found so difficult to handle, dominated the writer's correspondence between 1887 and 1889, more than any other play, and prompted a great deal of revision, draft after draft, seeking to make his intentions clear without killing the essential mystery at the heart of any work of art.

Not for the first or last time, Chekhov was accused in some quarters of a sort of cynical moral neutrality. His response, at this stage of his development as a dramatist, was to have Ivanov address the audience directly, and over the winter of 1888 he extensively rewrote the play, in particular inserting a long soliloquy in Act III, a key speech in which Ivanov is unsparing in his self-abnegation, and no more able than Dr Lvov or anyone else to explain it. Chekhov was also aware that his female characters, including Sasha, were rather under-developed, as for the most part they remain in later drafts; the grasping Zinaida, Avdotya and Mrs Babakin are essentially two-dimensional, and might have stepped out of the pages of Ostrovsky, whose bourgeois comedies were a repertoire staple in the young Chekhov's local theatre at Taganrog.

Sasha was a different matter, and there is evidence in Chekhov's letters that he intended a somewhat negative function for her. In the 1887 version, Ivanov appears to regard her as the daughter he never had, and she makes only a minor contribution to the dénouement. By the time he felt in a position to offer the play in St Petersburg, however, his liking for the vivacious young actress, M. G. Savina, who played Sasha, counterpoised by his increasing dissatisfaction with Davydov's Ivanov, resulted in a significant expansion of her role. For example, in a later draft, cut from the *Collected Works* text, Chekhov inserted a playful courtship scene between the pair.

Among other changes, a few of Shabelsky's more offensive anti-Semitic jibes were cut, though there is anecdotal evidence that provincial audiences occasionally supplied their own, incensed at Chekhov's sympathetic portrayal of Anna Petrovna. Another plot strand, in which Dr Lvov confessed his love for Anna Petrovna, was wisely cut from the final version, leaving him motivation-free, as it were, apart from self-righteousness.

Audiences in 1887, however, like Chekhov himself, found Act IV of *Ivanov* least satisfactory, and a wholesale rewrite was demanded. In the version premiered at the Korsh Theatre, Act IV was divided into two parts, before and after Ivanov's wedding to Sasha. Part I treads water to an extent, in a manner foreign to the later Chekhov, and much of the dialogue is given over to desultory chit-chat about Ivanov's finances, Sasha's dowry, Shabelsky's relationship with the widow Babakin, etc., until the key confrontation between Ivanov and Sasha. In this version, the tone is significantly lighter, and Sasha, a little unconvincingly, cajoles Ivanov out of his determination to call off the wedding.

Part II, the aftermath of the ceremony, is distinctly jolly, with the less complex characters – Avdotya, Borkin, the widow Babakin and others, occupying the foreground with entertaining but essentially lightweight banter. And almost incredibly, the Ivanov who in the 1889 version 'never once smiled' at his fiancée, is presented here as ecstatically happy, at least until the arrival of Dr Lvov, the spectre at the feast, whose impassioned denunciation causes Ivanov to drop dead from shock. Small wonder, then, that Chekhov's first audiences found this ending problematic, or that the author should have felt the need to change the 1887 title page from 'comedy' to 'drama' in its later radical recension.

Thanks to Chekhov's extensive correspondence on *Ivanov*, as he worked his way through at least four drafts, a fascinating picture of the dramatist as critic has emerged, such as one could only wish for in that other, even more radical transmutation, from *The Wood Demon* to *Uncle Vanya*.

Ivanov: Stage History

Ivanov was first staged in provincial Saratov, a few days before it opened on 19 November 1887 in the Korsh theatre in Moscow. For the reasons already noted, Chekhov regarded the play as a failure, and it was taken off after only three performances. Two years later, the reconstructed *Ivanov* opened at the Imperial Alexandrinsky Theatre in St Petersburg, on 31 January 1889. On this occasion, the play was a resounding success, and enjoyed a substantial two-week run, to be revived at the Alexandrinsky in September of that same year, before transferring to the Korsh Theatre in Moscow, finally touring to Kiev and Odessa, and several other provincial centres.

Ivanov was eventually staged by the Moscow Art Theatre, under the direction of Nemirovich-Danchenko, in October 1904, with Stanislavsky as Shabelsky, and Olga Knipper as Anna Petrovna. Chekhov unfortunately was no longer there to witness it, having died in July of that year, but the production remained in the MAT repertoire until 1924. Chekhov's reputation declined to some degree after the October Revolution, when the travails endured by his middle-class characters seemed impossibly remote from those of his audiences. However, as part of the centennial celebrations in 1960, the Moscow Maly Theatre staged its first full-length Chekhov, a lively and fast-moving revival of *Ivanov*, directed by Boris Babochkin, who also played the title role. In 1976, a seminal production by Oleg Yefremov at the Moscow Art Theatre starred Innokenty Smoktunovsky, internationally admired by film buffs as an outstanding Hamlet, precisely catching the mood of the Brezhnev years, known to Russians as the 'period of stagnation'.

Until recently, stagings of *Ivanov* in England have been rare. The first production, by the Incorporated Stage Society, using a translation by Marian Fell, took place in December

1925 at the Duke of York's Theatre, London, directed by
Fyodor Komisarzhevsky. There appears to have been little
interest in the play thereafter, at least until John Fernald's
production, premiered on 20 April 1950 at the Arts Theatre,
with Michael Hordern as Ivanov. John Gielgud's production,
based on Ariadne Nicolaeff's translation and premiered at
the Phoenix Theatre on 30 September 1965, had Gielgud
himself in the title role, Yvonne Mitchell as Anna Petrovna,
and Claire Bloom as Sasha. Since then, *Ivanov* has steadily
become established in the English Chekhov repertoire, and
worthy of note are David Jones's 1976 staging at the
Aldwych Theatre, with John Wood as Ivanov, and Toby
Robertson's at the Old Vic, premiered on 14 August 1978,
and starring Derek Jacobi. Important productions in the
past two decades include Elijah Moshinsky's, in Ronald
Harwood's version, premiered at the Yvonne Arnaud
Theatre on 7 February 1989, later transferring to the Strand,
with Alan Bates as Ivanov and Felicity Kendal as Anna
Petrovna. David Hare's adaptation opened at the Almeida
Theatre, London, on 19 February 1997, directed by
Jonathan Kent, with Ralph Fiennes as Ivanov, and Harriet
Walter as Anna Petrovna. The National Theatre production
of David Harrower's translation, premiered at the Cottesloe
on 16 September 2002, directed by Katie Mitchell, and
featuring Owen Teale, Robert Bowman and Juliet Aubrey,
was widely acclaimed. More recently, Michael Grandage's
production of Tom Stoppard's version opened at the
Wyndham's Theatre as part of the Donmar West End
season on 17 September 2008, with Kenneth Branagh as
Ivanov, Gina McKee as Anna Petrovna and Tom Hiddleston
as Dr Lvov.

For Further Reading

Among biographies of Chekhov, Ronald Hingley's *A New Life of Chekhov*, Oxford University Press, 1976, is outstanding not only for its wealth of detail, but also the care the author takes to disentangle the man from the work. Also recommended are Ernest J. Simmon's *Chekhov: A Biography*, University of Chicago Press, 1962, and Donald Rayfield's *Chekhov: A Life*, Harper Collins, 1997. The same author's *Chekhov: The Evolution of his Art*, Barnes and Noble, New York, 1975, Maurice Valency's *The Breaking String*, Oxford University Press, 1966, and David Magarshack's *The Real Chekhov*, George Allen & Unwin, 1972, remain among the most perceptive and readable studies of the plays, joined by Richard Gilman's excellent *Chekhov's Plays: An Opening into Eternity*, Yale University Press, 1995. Nick Worrall's pocket-sized *File on Chekhov*, Methuen, 1986, is both a compact introduction to Chekhov's theatre, and a useful source of review material. *Anton Chekhov Rediscovered*, edited by Senderovich and Sendich, Russian Language Journal, 1987, includes a comprehensive bibliography of works in English relating to Chekhov, and *A Chekhov Companion*, edited by Toby W. Clyman, Greenwood Press, 1985, contains useful articles on themes ranging from social conditions in late nineteenth-century Russia, to the critical tradition, both native and Western. Chekhov's reception in the West, over the period roughly 1900–45, is also documented in detail by Viktor Emeljanow, in *Chekhov, the Critical Heritage*, Routledge & Kegan Paul, 1981. Patrick

Miles's *Chekhov on the British Stage*, Cambridge University Press, 1993, is a collection of essays by several hands, and contains a chronology of British productions of Chekhov up to 1991. More recently, *The Cambridge Companion to Chekhov*, eds. Vera Gottlieb and Paul Allain, Cambridge University Press, 2000, is an invaluable anthology of essays on a wide range of topics. Finally, on *Ivanov* specifically, Vol. II of *The Oxford Chekhov*, translated and edited by Ronald Hingley, and containing *Platonov*, *Ivanov* and *The Seagull*, Oxford University Press, 1967, includes a detailed account of Chekhov's various drafts of the play, and the full texts of both the 1887 and 1889 versions.

Chekhov: Key Dates

1860 Born 17 January in Taganrog, a port on the Sea of Azov.

1875 Father's grocery business fails, family flees to Moscow, leaving Chekhov behind.

1879 Completes his education at the local high school, and sets off for Moscow, to enter the Medical Faculty of Moscow University.

1880 First comic story published in 'The Dragonfly', a St Petersburg weekly.

1884 Graduates from university, begins medical practice in Moscow. First symptoms of tuberculosis.

1885 Contributes short stories to the 'St Petersburg Gazette' and 'New Time'.

1886 First collection: *Motley Tales*.

1887 Second collection: *In the Twilight*. First performance of *Ivanov* at the Korsh Theatre, Moscow, 19 November.

1888 First major story, *The Steppe*, published in the 'Northern Herald'. Awarded Pushkin Prize for Literature, by the Imperial Academy of Sciences.

1889 Revised draft of *Ivanov* premiered at Alexandrinsky Theatre, St Petersburg, 31 January. First performance of *The Wood Demon* at Abramova's Theatre, Moscow, 27 December.

1890 Travels across Siberia to carry out research on the penal colony of Sakhalin Island.

1896 Disastrous first performance of *The Seagull*, at the Alexandrinsky Theatre in St Petersburg, 17 October.

1898 Begins association with the Moscow Art Theatre. Worsening tuberculosis forces him to move to Yalta. On 17 December, first successful performance of *The Seagull*, by the Moscow Art Theatre.

1899 First Moscow performance of *Uncle Vanya*, by the same company, 26 October. Publication begins of his *Collected Works*, in ten volumes.

1901 First performance of *Three Sisters*, 31 January. Marries the Moscow Art Theatre actress, Olga Knipper.

1903 Publishes last short story, *The Betrothed*.

1904 First performance of *The Cherry Orchard*, 17 January. Dies in Badenweiler, Germany, 2 July.

IVANOV

A Drama in Four Acts

Characters

IVANOV, *Nikolai Alekseyevich, permanent member of the Council for Peasant Affairs*

ANNA PETROVNA, *his wife, born Sarra Abramson*

SHABELSKY, *Count Matvei Semyonovich, his maternal uncle*

LEBEDEV, *Pavel Kirillych, chairman of the zemstvo (elective district council)*

ZINAIDA *Savishna, his wife*

SASHA, *the Lebedevs' daughter, aged twenty*

LVOV, *Yevgeny Konstantinovich, a young country doctor*

MRS BABAKIN, *Marfa Yegorovna, a young widow, landowner and daughter of a wealthy merchant*

KOSYKH, *Dmitry Nikitich, an excise officer*

BORKIN, *Mikhail Mikhailovich, a distant relative of Ivanov, his estate manager*

AVDOTYA *Nazarovna, an old woman of unspecified profession*

YEGORUSHKA, *a hanger-on of the Lebedevs*

PYOTR, *Ivanov's manservant*

GAVRILA, *the Lebedevs' manservant*

Various other GUESTS *and* SERVANTS

The action takes place in one of the provinces of Central Russia.

ACT ONE

The garden of IVANOV's *estate. At left, the front of the house, with a veranda. One window is open. In front of the house, a wide semi-circular area, from which paths lead off right and centre to other parts of the garden. At right, some garden seats and small tables, on one of which a lamp is burning. Evening is drawing on. As the curtain rises, a piano and cello duet can be heard from inside the house.*

IVANOV *is sitting at a table reading a book.* BORKIN *appears at the bottom of the garden in top-boots, carrying a hunting rifle. He is a little drunk. Catching sight of* IVANOV, *he tiptoes up to him and points the gun at his head.*

IVANOV (*starts up in alarm*). Misha, for God's sake! You gave me a fright. I've got enough on my plate without your silly jokes. (*Sits down again.*) I suppose you think that's funny.

BORKIN (*chuckling*). Alright, alright, I'm sorry. (*Sits down beside him.*) I won't do it again, I promise. (*Takes off his cap.*) Phew, it's hot! Would you believe – I've just ridden fifteen miles in under three hours? I'm worn out. Look, feel that – that's my heart pounding.

IVANOV (*reading his book*). Yes, fine – later.

BORKIN. No, listen. Feel, right now. (*Takes* IVANOV's *hand and places it on his chest.*) You hear that? Ba-boom, ba-boom, ba-boom . . . That's a sign of heart trouble, that is. I could drop dead any minute. Would it upset you, d'you think, if I died?

IVANOV. Not now – I'm trying to read.

BORKIN. No, but seriously – would you be upset, if I suddenly dropped dead? Nikolai Alekseyevich, would you be upset if I died?

IVANOV. Oh, stop pestering me!

BORKIN. My dear, just tell me – would it upset you?

IVANOV. You're reeking of vodka, *that's* what upsets me! It's disgusting, Misha.

BORKIN (*laughs*). Am I really? Well, that *is* a surprise. Actually, there's nothing surprising about it. I happened to bump into the magistrate in Plesniki, and the pair of us, would you believe, downed about eight vodkas each. And not to put too fine a point on it, drinking's bad for you. I mean, isn't it? Eh? It's bad for you, right?

IVANOV. Oh, this is intolerable! You're doing this deliberately to annoy me, Misha.

BORKIN. Alright, I'm sorry, I'm sorry. Sit down, for goodness' sake. (*Stands up, makes to exit.*) Honestly, some people – you can't even have a word with them! (*Comes back.*) Oh yes, I almost forgot . . . Eighty-two roubles, please.

IVANOV. What eighty-two roubles?

BORKIN. To pay the workmen tomorrow.

IVANOV. I haven't got it.

BORKIN. Well, thank you most humbly! (*Mimicking him.*) 'I haven't got it.' I mean, the men have to be paid. Haven't they?

IVANOV. I don't know. I've got nothing today. If you can wait till the first of the month, till I get my salary.

BORKIN. You know, it's a waste of time even discussing these things with you. The men'll be here for their money tomorrow morning, not the first of the month!

IVANOV. So what do you want me to do? You keep nagging me, you're worse than toothache. And you have a nasty habit of badgering me just when I've started to read or write or whatever . . .

BORKIN. I'm asking you – do the men get paid or not? Oh, this is pointless! (*Waves his hands dismissively.*) Huh, landowners, gentlemen farmers – the hell with the lot of them! Call themselves agriculturists – three thousand acres and not a penny to show for it! Like having a wine-cellar and no corkscrew! Well, I'll just have to sell the horse and cart tomorrow. Yes, sir, I might just do that. I've already sold the oats before they're even harvested, and I'll do the same tomorrow with the rye. (*Paces up and down the stage.*) You think I won't? Well, sir, if that's what you think, you've got the wrong man.

SHABELSKY *and* ANNA PETROVNA *are inside the house meanwhile, and* SHABELSKY *is heard through the open window.*

SHABELSKY. Really, it's quite impossible trying to play with you! You've no ear for music, and your touch is dreadful. You're about as sensitive as a stuffed pike!

ANNA P (*appearing at the open window*). Who was that talking just now? Was that you, Misha? What are you doing, pacing up and down like that?

BORKIN. It's that *Monsieur Nicolas* of yours – he'd drive
  you to it!

ANNA P. Listen, Misha – tell the servants to cart some hay
  over to the croquet lawn.

BORKIN (*with a dismissive wave*). Oh, leave me in peace . . .

ANNA P. You know, that's no way to talk, it does nothing
  for you. Not if you want to be a hit with the ladies. You
  shouldn't ever let them see you in a bad mood, or on
  your high horse. (*To her husband.*) Come on, Nikolai, let's
  go and tumble in the hay!

IVANOV. Anna, it's not good for your health, standing at
  that open window. Go back in, please do. (*Shouts.*) Uncle,
  close the window! (*The window is closed.*)

BORKIN. And don't forget you've to pay the interest to
  Lebedev, day after tomorrow.

IVANOV. Yes, I know. I'm going over to Lebedev's later
  today, and I'll ask him if he'd mind waiting . . . (*Looks at
  his watch.*)

BORKIN. So when are you going?

IVANOV. In a minute.

BORKIN. No, hold on, wait! It's Sasha's birthday today,
  isn't it. (*Tuts.*) I almost forgot. Honestly, what a memory.
  (*Springs to his feet.*) I'll come! Yes, I'll come with you.
  (*Sings.*) I'll come with you! I'll have a bath, chew some
  paper, with three drops of ammonia, and I'll be as right
  as rain. Dear Nikolai Alekseyevich – God love you, my
  angel, but you're a bundle of nerves, down in the dumps

all the time, complaining. I mean, just think of the things we could do together, you and I, there'd be no stopping us! And I'd do anything for you, you know that. Would you like me to marry the widow Babakin? You can have half of her dowry, it's yours. No, take all of it – take the lot, damn it!

IVANOV. Don't talk such rubbish!

BORKIN. No, I'm serious. Do you want me to marry her, young Marfa? Split the dowry fifty-fifty? But why am I telling you this, you're not even listening. (*Mimicking him.*) 'Don't talk such rubbish!' You know, you're a decent fellow, quite intelligent, but there's something lacking, some sort of vital spark. You should break out once in a while, and to hell with the consequences. You're neurotic, forever whining – yet if you were a normal person, you could make a million in a year. For instance, if I had two thousand, three hundred roubles right now, I'd have twenty thousand in two weeks' time. You don't believe me? I'm still talking rubbish? Alright, then, give me twenty-three hundred roubles, and within a week I'll make twenty thousand for you. Ovsyanov's selling a strip of land, right opposite ours, for twenty-three hundred. If we buy that land, both banks of the river'll belong to us. And if we own both banks, we'll be entitled to dam the river. Right? So we can start building a mill, and the minute word gets round that we're planning to dam the river, all the people downstream'll raise merry hell, and we'll just tell them straight – if you don't want a dam, you'll have to cough up. D'you follow me? The Zarevsky factory – let's say five thousand; the Korolkov, three thousand; the monastery, five thousand . . .

IVANOV. That's sharp practice, Misha. Keep your
   thoughts to yourself, unless you want an argument.

BORKIN (*sits down at the table*). Yes, of course – I might've
   known. You're not prepared to do anything, and my
   hands are tied.

Enter SHABELSKY *and* LVOV *from the house.*

SHABELSKY. Doctors are like lawyers, with one difference.
   Lawyers rob you blind, but doctors rob you blind,
   then murder you . . . Present company excepted, of
   course. (*Sits down on a garden seat.*) Yes, charlatans and
   exploiters . . . Maybe in some ideal world, you might
   bump into a few exceptions to the rule, but . . . in the
   course of a lifetime I must've paid out twenty thousand
   roubles in doctor's fees, and I've never met one yet who
   didn't strike me as a licensed swindler.

BORKIN (*to* IVANOV.) Yes, you won't do anything, and
   my hands are tied. That's why we've no money . . .

SHABELSKY. I'll say again, I'm not talking about present
   company . . . Maybe there are exceptions, although,
   generally speaking . . . (*Yawns.*)

IVANOV (*closing his book*). Well, Doctor?

LVOV (*looking back at the window*). Same as I said this
   morning: she needs to go to the Crimea as soon as
   possible. (*Pacing up and down.*)

SHABELSKY (*with a snort of laughter*). Crimea! . . . Why
   don't you and I take up medicine, Misha? It's a piece of
   cake . . . Madame So-and-so gets a tickle in her throat,
   starts coughing out of sheer boredom, and we take a

piece of paper, apply our science, and prescribe as
follows: first, one young doctor, then a trip to the
Crimea, where some handsome young Tartar . . .

IVANOV (*to* SHABELSKY). Oh, don't be such a bore! (*To*
LVOV.) Trips to the Crimea cost money. And supposing
I can find the money, she'll almost certainly refuse to go.

LVOV. Yes, I know. (*A pause.*)

BORKIN. Listen, Doctor – seriously, is Anna Petrovna so
ill that she has to go to the Crimea?

LVOV (*looks round at the window*). Yes . . . tuberculosis.

BORKIN. Phew! That's bad. Actually, the way she looks,
I've thought for some time she wouldn't last long.

LVOV. Anyway . . . keep your voice down. They can hear
you inside. (*A pause.*)

BORKIN (*sighs*). You know, this life of ours . . . A man's life
is like a little flower, blossoming in a meadow. Along
comes a goat, and eats it – no more flower.

SHABELSKY. Nonsense. Nonsense, and more nonsense . . .
(*Yawns.*) Piffle and balderdash. (*A pause.*)

BORKIN. Meanwhile, gentlemen, I've just been instructing
Nikolai Alekseyevich on how to get his hands on some
money. I've given him a brilliant idea, but my seed's fallen
on stony ground, same as usual. You can't get through to
the man. I mean, just look at him – the picture of
melancholy, spleen, depression, downright misery . . .

SHABELSKY (*stands up and stretches*). You're a regular
brainbox, ever ready with some wonderful idea, teaching

us all how to live – well, I wish you really *did* have
something to teach me, just once. So come on, clever
clogs, show me a way out of this mess . . .

BORKIN (*stands up*). I'm going for a swim. Goodbye,
gentlemen . . . (*To* SHABELSKY.) You have at least
twenty ways out. Put me in your place for a week, and
I'd have twenty thousand. (*Goes out.*)

SHABELSKY (*following him out*). What do you mean? Well,
come on, show me.

BORKIN. There's nothing to show. It's quite simple . . .
(*Turns back.*) Right, Nikolai Alekseyevich, give me a
rouble.

IVANOV *gives him a rouble in silence.*

Merci! You know, you still hold all the aces.

SHABELSKY (*follows him out*). How come?

BORKIN. I tell you, if I was in your position for a week,
I'd have thirty thousand, if not more. (*Goes out with*
SHABELSKY.)

IVANOV (*after a pause*). Idle people, idle talk – having to
answer their stupid questions – I'm sick and tired of it,
Doctor, I really am. I've become extremely irritable and
bad-tempered. I'm so abrupt with people these days I
scarcely recognise myself. My head aches for days on
end, I can't sleep, and there's a persistent ringing in my
ears. What's more, there's nothing I can do for it.
Nothing whatsoever.

LVOV. Nikolai Alekseyevich, I need to have a serious talk
with you.

IVANOV. Go ahead.

LVOV. It's about Anna Petrovna. (*Sits down.*) She won't agree to the Crimean trip, but she would go if you went with her.

IVANOV (*after some thought*). It would cost too much, the two of us. Besides which, they won't give me extended leave. I've already had a holiday this year.

LVOV. Well, I daresay that's so. But the fact remains, the only real remedy for tuberculosis is absolute rest, and your wife doesn't get a moment's peace here. She's in a state of nerves constantly, because of the way you treat her. You'll have to excuse me, if I'm getting a little heated, but I'll be blunt – the way you're behaving is killing her. (*A pause.*) I wish I had a higher opinion of you, Nikolai Alekseyevich.

IVANOV. That's true, I suppose. I'm very much at fault, but I'm terribly confused – it's as if I'm sunk in inertia, and for the life of me, I can't understand it. It's a mystery to me – I just don't understand other people, or myself. (*Looks up at the window.*) They can hear us, let's go for a walk. (*They stand up.*) You're a good friend, and I'd like to tell you the whole story from the beginning, but it's so long and complicated, it would take all night. (*They walk on.*) Anna is a quite extraordinary woman, most unusual . . . She changed her religion for my sake, left her mother and father, and walked away from a fortune, and if I'd asked her to make a hundred more sacrifices, she would have done so without batting an eyelid. Well now, I'm not in the least extraordinary, and I've sacrificed nothing. Anyway, it's a long story . . . The

fact of the matter, my dear Doctor . . . (*Clearly uncomfortable.*)
The fact is . . . Well, to put it in a nutshell – when I
married her, I loved her passionately, and swore to love
her for ever, but now, five years on, while she still loves
me, I . . . (*Throws up his hands.*) I mean, here you are,
telling me she's going to die soon, and I feel neither love
nor pity, just a sort of emptiness, exhaustion. To an
onlooker, this must seem terrible. I don't understand it
myself, I've no idea what's going on in my mind. (*They
go out down the garden path.*)

SHABELSKY (*enters from the house, laughing*). Well, honest to
God, he's no ordinary crook – the man's a genius, a
virtuoso! They should put up a monument to him. He's
a combination of every sort of modern nastiness –
lawyer, doctor, banker, gangster. (*Sits down on the bottom
step of the veranda.*) And it's not as if he'd studied
anywhere, that's the amazing thing. Just think what a
master criminal he'd have become if he'd had a bit of
education, read the classics and so forth! You could have
twenty thousand inside a week, he says – you still hold
all the aces, he says, being as you've got a title. (*Laughs.*)
Any girl with a dowry would marry you . . .

ANNA PETROVNA *opens the window, and looks down.*

Do you want me to fix you up with Marfa? he says. Who
on earth is Marfa? Oh, her, the Balabalkin girl – yes,
Balabalkin – the one that looks like a washerwoman.

ANNA P. Is that you, Count?

SHABELSKY. Yes, what is it?

ANNA PETROVNA *laughs.*

(*Affects a Jewish accent.*) Vot are you leffink at, eh?

ANNA P. I've just remembered one of your sayings. You
remember, when you were talking at dinner? Something
about a thief, and a horse . . . What was it again?

SHABELSKY. Oh, yes.

'A baptised Jew,
A thief's remorse
Ring as true
As a spavined horse . . . '

ANNA P (*laughs*). You can't tell even the simplest riddle
without saying something nasty. You're a wicked man.
(*Gravely.*) Joking aside, Count, you're quite evil. It's
upsetting, living with you, and frankly a bore. You do
nothing but complain – everybody's either a fool or a
knave, according to you. Tell me honestly, Count, have
you ever had a good word for anybody?

SHABELSKY. What's this – some kind of interrogation?

ANNA P. You know, we've been living under the same roof
now for five years, and I've never once heard you speak
about people in a normal way, without mocking them,
or sneering at them. What harm have they done you?
Do you seriously think you're better than everyone else?

SHABELSKY. Not in the least. I'm as nasty a piece of
work as the next man, irredeemably vulgar and only fit
for the scrapheap, like an old shoe. I'm forever doing
myself down – I mean, who am I? What am I? I used to
be rich, free, and moderately happy, but now . . . I'm a

hanger-on, a parasite, a figure of fun. If I get indignant, or contemptuous, people just laugh at me. And when I laugh, they nod their heads sagely: oh, the old man's off his rocker. Most of the time, they don't even listen to me, or acknowledge my presence.

ANNA P (*calmly*). That's him hooting again . . .

SHABELSKY. Who is?

ANNA P. The owl. He hoots every night.

SHABELSKY. Let it hoot all it wants. Things can't get any worse. (*Stretches.*) Ah, my dear Sarra, if I won a hundred or two hundred thousand roubles, I'd show you a thing or two! You wouldn't see me for dust. I'd be out of this hole so fast – no more free meals and handouts – and I wouldn't set foot here again until the crack of doom.

ANNA P. And what would you do if you did win?

SHABELSKY (*after some thought*). First of all, I'd go to Moscow, to hear a gypsy band. After that . . . After that, I'd shoot off to Paris – I'd rent an apartment there, and go to the Russian church . . .

ANNA P. Then what?

SHABELSKY. Then I'd go and sit by my wife's graveside for days on end, and just think about things. I'd sit there, by her grave, till I died. My wife's buried in Paris . . . (*A pause.*)

ANNA P. This is terribly boring. Shall we play another duet?

SHABELSKY. Alright – set up the music.

IVANOV (*appears on the garden path with* LVOV). My dear
   Doctor Lvov, you left university only last year, you're still
   young and full of life, but I'm thirty-five, so I have the
   right to give you some advice. Don't ever marry a
   Jewess, a neurotic, or a bluestocking. Choose someone
   nice and nondescript, colourless and unfussy. Organise
   your whole life around the conventions, and the more
   grey and monotonous the background, the better. Don't
   take on the world single-handed, don't tilt at windmills,
   or beat your head against a brick wall. And may God
   preserve you from all such things as scientific farming,
   'alternative' schools, and inflammatory speeches. Creep
   into your shell, and perform your own little God-given
   task. That's far more comfortable, more honest and
   healthier. But the life I've lived – it's been so exhausting,
   so draining! So many mistakes, and injustices, so many
   absurdities. (*Catching sight of* SHABELSKY, *suddenly
   irritated.*) Uncle, you're always hanging about, a man
   can't have a private conversation.

SHABELSKY (*tearfully*). Oh, for God's sake! A man can't
   get a minute's peace! (*Runs out into the house.*)

IVANOV (*calls after him*). Alright, I'm sorry! I'm sorry!
   (*To* LVOV.) Why did I have to offend him? I'm definitely
   losing my grip. I'll need to do something about it, I really
   will . . .

LVOV (*agitated*). Nikolai Alekseyevich, I've listened to you,
   and I'm sorry, but I'm going to be blunt. The way you
   speak, your very tone of voice, let alone what you
   actually say, is so self-centred and unfeeling, so cold and
   heartless . . . Someone very close to you is dying, her
   days are numbered, and you . . . You can be so unloving,

you walk around, dispensing advice, posturing . . . I can't express myself, I'm not very good with words, but . . . I dislike you intensely!

IVANOV. Well, that's as maybe. You're on the sidelines, of course . . . It's quite possible you understand me – probable, in fact, and I'm sorry, I truly am. (*Listens.*) I think they're bringing the carriage round. I'd better go in and get changed. (*Goes towards the house and stops.*) You don't like me, Doctor, and you don't try to conceal it. Your heart's in the right place. (*Goes into the house.*)

LVOV (*alone*). Oh, I'm so damn spineless! That's another opportunity let slip, I should've gone for the jugular. I just can't speak to him calmly, in cold blood. I've only got to open my mouth to say something, and right away I start puffing and panting (*Indicates his chest.*), and get completely tongue-tied. I loathe this damned hypocrite, this self-centred pious fraud, with all my heart . . . And now he's going out. Meanwhile, his wretched wife's only happiness is when he's by her side – she dotes on him, begs him to spend even one evening at home, but he can't, he just can't. It's too confining, too claustrophobic. If he had to spend an evening at home, he'd put a bullet in his head, out of sheer boredom. Poor man – he needs space, so he can get involved in some new dirty tricks. Oh, don't think I don't know why you go out every night to the Lebedevs'! I know alright!

SHABELSKY, IVANOV *and* ANNA PETROVNA *emerge from the house.* IVANOV *is wearing his hat and overcoat.*

SHABELSKY. Really, Nikolai, this is monstrous! You're out every night, and we're stuck here alone. We go to bed at eight o'clock from sheer boredom, it's inhuman, you can't call it a life. And why is it you can go out, and we can't? Why?

ANNA P. Leave him, Count – just let him go . . .

IVANOV (*to his wife*). How can you go out? You're too ill. You're not well, and you're not supposed to be outdoors after sunset – just ask the doctor. You're not a child, Anna, you've got to be sensible. (*To* SHABELSKY.) And why do you want to go?

SHABELSKY. I'd rather fry in hell, or be eaten by crocodiles, than stay in this place. I'm bored rigid. Everybody's fed up with me. You leave me here in the house so she won't be bored on her own, but I just get on her nerves, nagging her all the time.

ANNA P. Leave him be, Count – leave him! Let him go, if that's what'll make him happy.

IVANOV. I don't know why you're taking that tone, Anna, I'm not going there to enjoy myself, you know. I need to talk to them about money.

ANNA P. I don't understand why you have to justify yourself. Just go – nobody's holding you back.

IVANOV. Oh God, why are we doing this to each other? Is this really necessary?

SHABELSKY (*tearfully*). Nikolai, dear Nikolai – take me with you, please! Just to have a quick look at all those knaves and fools, it'll maybe cheer me up. I mean, I haven't been anywhere since Easter!

IVANOV (*irritably*). Alright, damn it, let's go! Honestly, you all make me sick.

SHABELSKY. Really? Well, *merci*! *Merci!* (*Delightedly seizes IVANOV by the arm, and takes him aside.*) Can I wear your straw hat?

IVANOV. Yes, yes, just hurry up, will you?

SHABELSKY *runs into the house.*

I'm fed up with the lot of you. Oh God, what am I saying? This is impossible, I shouldn't talk like this to you, Anna. We never used to be like this. Anyway, goodbye, Anna, I'll be back by one.

ANNA P. Kolya, darling, please stay at home.

IVANOV (*troubled*). Oh, my poor, dear darling – please, please don't try and stop me going out in the evenings. It's cruel of me, I know, it's very unfair, but please, just let me be unfair. It's sheer torture for me to stay at home. The minute the sun goes down, I start to get depressed. Seriously depressed! Don't ask me why, I don't know myself. I swear to you, I don't know. I get depressed here, and when I go over to the Lebedevs', it's even worse. I come back home, and I'm depressed again. It's like that the whole night, it's absolutely desperate.

ANNA P. Then why don't you stay home, Nikolai? We'll sit and talk, the way we used to – have supper together, read a book. Your uncle and I have been learning a lot of duets, to play for you. (*Puts her arms around him.*) Please stay! (*A pause.*) I don't understand you. This has been going on for a whole year now. Why have you changed?

IVANOV. I don't know, I don't know.

ANNA P. Why don't you want me to go out with you in the evenings?

IVANOV. Well, if you really must know, I'll tell you. It's a harsh thing to say, but it's better I do. When I get depressed like that, I start . . . Well, I start not to love you. At times like that, I've got to escape, even from you. To cut a long story short, I need to get out of the house.

ANNA P. Depressed? That I can well understand. You know something, Kolya? You should try singing, laughing, or even just getting angry, the way you used to. Stay in, and we'll laugh, and drink some homebrew – that'll get rid of your depression in no time. I could sing to you if you like. Or we could go and sit in your study in the dark, the way we used to, and you could tell me all about your depression. Your eyes are so full of suffering! I'll look into them and start crying, and then we'll both feel better. (*Laughs, and then starts to cry.*) What do you think, Kolya? Flowers come round again every spring, but happiness never does – is that it? Yes? Oh, go on, go on out . . .

IVANOV. Pray to God for me, Anna. (*Makes to go out, stops, and thinks for a moment.*) No, no, I can't! (*Goes out.*)

ANNA P. Go on, then! (*Sits down at the table.*)

LVOV (*pacing up and down the stage*). Anna Petrovna, you really must make it a rule – the minute the clock strikes six, you've got to go indoors, and not leave the house till the morning. It's too damp in the evenings, and it's bad for you.

ANNA P. Yes, master.

LVOV. What do you mean, 'Yes, master'? I'm serious.

ANNA P. But I don't want to be serious. (*Coughs.*)

LVOV. There, you see? You're coughing already.

SHABELSKY *emerges from the house, his hat and overcoat on.*

SHABELSKY. Where's Nikolai? Is the carriage ready?

Quickly goes over to ANNA PETROVNA, *and kisses her hand.*

Goodnight, my sweet. (*Pulls a face, affects Jewish accent.*)
Vot else can I do? Excuse, plis. (*Hurries out.*)

LVOV. Buffoon!

A pause. The sound of an accordion in the distance.

ANNA P. What a bore! The coachman and the cooks are
going out to a dance and I'm left behind, abandoned.
Doctor, what are you pacing up and down for? Sit down,
for goodness' sake.

LVOV. I can't sit still. (*A pause.*)

ANNA P. They're playing 'Greenfinch' in the kitchen.

Sings.

'Greenfinch, greenfinch, where have you been?
Drinking strong vodka down on the green . . .

A pause.

Doctor, are your mother and father still alive?

LVOV. My father's dead, my mother's still alive.

ANNA P. Do you ever miss your mother?

LVOV. I don't have the time.

ANNA P (*laughs*). Flowers bloom again every spring, but
     happiness never does. Who told me that saying? Now,
     let me think . . . Oh yes – I think it was actually Nikolai.
     (*Listens.*) There's that owl hooting again.

LVOV. Let him hoot.

ANNA P. You know, Doctor, I'm beginning to think I'm just
     unlucky. A lot of people, perhaps no better than me, can
     be happy, and pay nothing for their happiness. But I've
     had to pay for everything – absolutely everything! . . .
     And at such a price – why am I being charged such a
     frightful rate of interest? My dear friend, you're so
     careful with me, all of you, so tactful. You're afraid to
     tell me the truth but do you think I don't know what's
     wrong with me? I know all too well. Anyway, this is very
     boring. (*In a mock Jewish accent.*) Excuse, plis – heff you no
     chokes to tell me?

LVOV. I don't know any.

ANNA P. Nikolai does. And I'm beginning to wonder at the
     injustice of people: why don't they respond to love *with*
     love, why do they repay truth with lies? Tell me, how
     long are my mother and father going to carry on hating
     me? They live forty miles from here, and day and night,
     even in my sleep, I can feel their hatred. And how am I
     to understand Nikolai's depression? He says it's only at
     night he doesn't love me, when his depression sets in.
     That I can understand and accept. But supposing he's
     stopped loving me altogether? That's not possible, of

course, but just suppose . . . ? No, no, I mustn't even
think about it. (*Sings.*) 'Greenfinch, greenfinch, where
have you been . . . ' (*Shudders.*) The terrible thoughts I
have! You're not married, Doctor, there's a lot you don't
understand . . .

LVOV. You say you wonder . . . (*Sits down beside her.*) No, no –
I wonder . . . I wonder about *you*! I mean, just explain to
me, tell me how a decent, clever, almost saintly woman
like you, can let herself be so blatantly deceived, and
dragged off to this godforsaken owls' nest? What are you
doing here? What have you in common with this cold-
hearted, soulless . . . No, let's leave your husband out of
this. Just where do you fit in to this sterile, pointless
environment? Good God almighty! This lunatic Count
with his interminable whining, that crook Borkin, prince
of thieves, with his detestable ugly mug! Just tell me,
please, what the hell are you doing here? How did you
wind up in this place?

ANNA P (*laughs*). That's exactly how he used to speak, just
like that. But his eyes are bigger, and whenever he got
heated about something, they fairly blazed – keep
talking! Go on!

LVOV (*stands up and waves his arms in despair*). What do you
want me to say? Look, go indoors, please.

ANNA P. You say Nikolai is this, that and the next thing.
How do you know? Can you really know a person after
only six months? He's an extraordinary man, Doctor,
and I'm just sorry you didn't know him two or three
years ago. He's very depressed now, doesn't say, or do
much, but in the old days . . . he was such a charmer! I

fell in love with him at first sight. (*Laughs.*) Just one look, and I was absolutely smitten! He said, 'Let's go away!' – and I cut all my ties, like snipping off dead leaves, you know, and off I went . . . (*A pause.*) But now . . . now he goes out to the Lebedevs', to amuse himself with other women, while I sit out here in the garden, listening to owls screeching . . .

A nightwatchman's rattle is heard.

You have no brothers, then, Doctor?

LVOV. No.

ANNA PETROVNA *sobs.*

What is it? What's the matter?

ANNA P (*stands up*). I can't stand it, Doctor – I've got to go there.

LVOV. Go where?

ANNA P. Where he is. I'm going . . . Tell them to harness the horses. (*Runs into the house.*)

LVOV. No, I absolutely refuse! I can't practise medicine in these circumstances! Apart from the fact that I don't get paid, now they're riding roughshod over my feelings. No, I won't do it. Enough! (*Goes into the house.*)

Curtain.

ACT TWO

The ballroom in the Lebedevs' house, leading directly out to the garden; doors to left and right. Antique, expensive furniture. A chandelier, candelabra, and paintings, all under dust covers. ZINAIDA is seated on a settee; elderly female GUESTS are sitting in armchairs on either side of her; the younger GUESTS are sitting on chairs. Upstage, beside the exit to the garden, people are playing cards, including KOSYKH, AVDOTYA and YEGORUSHKA. GAVRILA is standing by the door at right, and the MAID is taking round a tray of snacks. Throughout the whole scene, GUESTS circulate to and from the garden, by the door at right. MRS BABAKIN enters through the door, right, and goes up to ZINAIDA.

ZINAIDA (*delightedly*). Marfa, darling!

MRS BABAKIN. Zinaida, how lovely! Congratulations on Sasha's birthday! (*They embrace.*) God bless you and . . .

ZINAIDA. Thank you, dear Marfa, I'm so happy . . . Tell me, how are you keeping?

MRS BABAKIN. Very well, thank you. (*Sits beside her on the settee.*) Good evening, all you young people!

The GUESTS stand up and bow.

FIRST GUEST (*laughs*). Young people? You're not old, surely?

MRS BABAKIN (*sighs*). We can't lay claim to be young these days . . .

FIRST GUEST (*laughing politely*). Oh, come now – you're a widow in name only. You could give all the young girls a run for their money.

GAVRILA *hands* MRS BABAKIN *a glass of tea*.

ZINAIDA (*to* GAVRILA). Not like that – what are you thinking of? Bring Mrs Babakin some jam – gooseberry or something.

MRS BABAKIN. No, no – don't bother, thanks. (*A pause.*)

FIRST GUEST. So, Mrs Babakin, did you come through Mushkino?

MRS BABAKIN. No, by the Zaimishche road – it's a much better way.

FIRST GUEST. Yes, indeed.

KOSYKH. Two spades.

YEGORUSHKA. Pass.

AVDOTYA. Pass.

SECOND GUEST. Pass.

MRS BABAKIN (*to* ZINAIDA). Lottery tickets are worth an absolute fortune now, darling. They're up to two hundred and seventy roubles for the first draw, and two fifty or so for the second – you've never heard anything like it.

ZINAIDA (*sighs*). Very nice, if you've got plenty of them.

MRS BABAKIN. I wouldn't say that, my dear. They may be worth a lot, but it's not a good idea to put your money into them. They cost the earth to insure.

ZINAIDA. Well, that's as maybe, my dear, but we live in hope. (*Sighs.*) And trust to God's mercy.

THIRD GUEST. The way I see it, *mesdames*, there's no point in having capital these days. Investments give you very little dividend, and lending money at interest is an extremely risky business. As I understand it, *mesdames*, a person with any capital nowadays is in a far worse position, *mesdames*, than someone . . .

MRS BABAKIN (*sighs*). That's very true!

FIRST GUEST *yawns.*

Should you be yawning in front of ladies?

FIRST GUEST. I do beg your pardon, *mesdames*, I didn't mean to.

ZINAIDA *stands up and goes out by the door at right. A prolonged silence.*

YEGORUSHKA. Two diamonds.

AVDOTYA. Pass.

SECOND GUEST. Pass.

KOSYKH. Pass.

MRS BABAKIN (*aside*). Oh God, this is so boring!

ZINAIDA (*re-entering by the door at right, along with* LEBEDEV, *quietly*). What were you doing, hiding out there? Really, what a cheek! Go and sit down with your guests. (*Sits back down on her former seat.*)

LEBEDEV (*yawns*). What a pain in the neck. (*Catching sight of* MRS BABAKIN.) Goodness me – it's our little sugar plum! (*Greets her.*) And how is your precious health, dear lady?

MRS BABAKIN. Very good, thank you.

LEBEDEV. Well, thank the Lord for that. (*Sits down in an armchair.*) Yes, indeed, yes. Gavrila!

GAVRILA *brings him a glass of vodka and a tumbler of water. He downs the vodka, and chases it with water.*

FIRST GUEST. Your good health!

LEBEDEV. Good health my eye! I'm just thankful I'm not six feet under! (*To his wife.*) Zina, where's our birthday girl?

KOSYKH (*wailing*). I don't believe this – we're cleaned out again! (*Leaps to his feet.*) Dammit to hell, how come we keep losing?

AVDOTYA (*jumps up, enraged*). What are you on about? If you don't know how to play, then don't! What d'you think you're doing, leading one of their suits? No wonder you were stuck with the ace! . . .

They both run round to the front of the table.

KOSYKH (*tearfully*). I beg your pardon – I had the ace, King, Queen, and eight diamonds, the ace of spades, one very small heart, for God's sake, and she couldn't manage even a small slam! I called no trumps . . .

AVDOTYA (*interrupting him*). No, it was me that called no trumps. You declared *two* no trumps!

KOSYKH. This is driving me mad! Look – you had . . . I had . . . you had . . . (*To* LEBEDEV.) Pavel Kirillych, you be the judge. See, look – I had diamonds – ace, King, Queen, and eight more diamonds . . .

LEBEDEV (*plugging his ears*). Oh, for God's sake, give it a rest!

AVDOTYA (*shouts*). And I called no trumps, I did!

KOSYKH (*fiercely*). God damn me for a miserable wretch, if I ever play cards again with that old crow!

He rushes out to the garden. The SECOND GUEST *follows him out, while* YEGORUSHKA *remains at the table.*

AVDOTYA. Phew! He's brought me out in a sweat. Old crow, indeed! And the same to you!

MRS BABAKIN. Well, you lost your temper too, my dear.

AVDOTYA (*catching sight of* MRS BABAKIN, *throws up her hands*). Ah, my lovely lady! She's here too, and I didn't even notice her. I must be going blind or something . . . Darling! (*Kisses her shoulder and sits down beside her.*) How delightful! Just let me have a look at you, you beautiful creature. Ssshh! Ssshh! That's enough – mustn't tempt fate.

LEBEDEV. Oh, don't overdo it – you'd do better to find her a husband!

AVDOTYA. And so I will! I won't lay my old bones to rest, sinner that I am, until I've married off her and Sasha both . . . No, I won't rest . . . (*Sighs.*) Only where are you supposed to find husbands these days, eh? Just look at them, sitting preening their feathers like a bunch of wet hens!

THIRD GUEST. That's a most inept comparison. The way I see it, *mesdames,* if today's young men prefer the bachelor life, it's because of the social milieu, so to speak . . .

LEBEDEV. Oh, spare us your theories – I can't be bothered with them.

SASHA enters and goes over to her father.

SASHA. Such a beautiful day, and you're all sitting sweltering indoors.

ZINAIDA. Sasha, darling, don't you see? Mrs Babakin's here.

SASHA. Oh, I'm sorry. (*Goes over and greets* MRS BABAKIN.)

MRS BABAKIN. So, you're too proud to come round and see me these days, even just to drop in? (*Kisses her.*) Many happy returns, my dear.

SASHA. Thank you. (*Sits down beside her father.*)

LEBEDEV. Yes, Avdotya, it's not easy finding a husband nowadays. Never mind bridegrooms, you can't even find a decent best man. Meaning no offence, but young men these days, God knows, they're a pretty spineless, milk-and-water lot. Can't dance, can't talk, can't even hold their drink.

AVDOTYA. Oh, they can do that alright, given half a chance.

LEBEDEV. Well, that's no great achievement – even horses can drink. No, I mean drink properly! Used to be in our

time, you'd knock your brains out at lectures the whole
day, and as soon as night fell you'd make a beeline for
the bright lights somewhere, and raise merry hell until
daybreak. And you'd dance, have some fun with the
girls, and there'd be a fair bit of this – (*Makes a drinking
gesture.*) Sometimes you'd just sit talking, putting the world
to rights, till all hours. But nowadays? Well, I don't
understand them – they're no use to man nor beast.
There's only one half-decent young man for miles around,
and he's already married. (*Sighs.*) And going off his head,
by all accounts.

MRS BABAKIN. Who's that?

LEBEDEV. Nikolai Ivanov.

MRS BABAKIN. Yes, he's a fine man. (*Pulls a long face.*)
Terribly unhappy, though.

ZINAIDA. Well, darling, you can hardly wonder. (*Sighs.*)
The poor man made a dreadful mistake. Married that
little Jewess, and fancied her parents would cough up a
tidy sum by way of dowry – quite wrongly, as it turned
out. The minute she changed her religion, they wanted
nothing more to do with her, and even laid a curse on
her. So he didn't get a penny. He regrets it now, but it's
too late.

SASHA. Mummy, that's not true.

MRS BABAKIN (*heatedly*). What do you mean not true,
Sasha? Everybody knows it. If it wasn't for her money,
why on earth would he marry a Jew? Aren't there
enough Russian girls? No, no, my dear, it was a mistake –
a bad mistake. (*Animatedly.*) And now he gives her a dog's

life, that's the funny part. The minute he gets home he wades into her – 'Your mother and father've cheated me – get to blazes out of my home!' But where can she go? Her parents won't have her. She could get a job as a maid somewhere, but she's not trained for anything. So he keeps on nagging her, till the Count has to step in. If it wasn't for the Count, he'd have done for her long ago.

AVDOTYA. Or he locks her in the cellar, and says, 'Eat garlic, damn you!' and she eats and eats, till she's about ready to burst! (*Laughs.*)

SASHA. Daddy, that's a downright lie!

LEBEDEV. Well, who cares? Let them say what they like. (*Shouts.*) Gavrila!

GAVRILA *brings him vodka and water.*

ZINAIDA. That's why the poor man's in such a bad way, my dear. His business has collapsed, and if Borkin didn't look after the farm, he and his little Jewess would have nothing to eat. (*Sighs.*) Yes, God alone knows what he's done to her! And we've suffered on his account as well, haven't we, my dear? I mean, would you believe, my dear, he's owed us nine thousand roubles for three years now!

MRS BABAKIN (*aghast*). Nine thousand!

ZINAIDA. Yes, my beloved husband arranged to lend it to him – he hasn't a clue who to lend money to, and who not. I'm not talking about the loan itself, but God help him, he can't even make the interest payments!

SASHA (*heatedly*). Mummy, you've said this a thousand times!

ZINAIDA. What business is it of yours? Why are you taking his side?

SASHA (*stands up*). And how do you have the nerve to speak like that about a person who's never done you any harm? What's he ever done to you?

THIRD GUEST. Miss Lebedev, if you'll allow me to say a word or two, I've always respected Mr Ivanov, and indeed been honoured to . . . But, well, strictly *entre nous*, I think the man's a bit of an opportunist.

SASHA. If that's what you think, good luck to you.

THIRD GUEST. Yes, well, I'll prove it to you – this was communicated to me by his guide and mentor, so to speak, a certain Mr Borkin. Two years ago, at the time of the cattle plague, he bought a number of cows and infected them . . .

ZINAIDA. Yes, yes, that's right! I remember that incident – I was told about it too.

THIRD GUEST. Anyway, he insured them – and you can take my word for it, he infected them with foot and mouth, and pocketed the insurance money.

SASHA. That's nonsense! Absolute rubbish! Nobody bought any cattle, or infected them! Borkin dreamed that one up himself, then went round bragging about it. And when Mr Ivanov found out, he made Borkin spend the next two weeks apologising. Mr Ivanov's only sorry that he hasn't the strength of character to get rid of Borkin, and that he's too trusting! He's been bled dry and swindled by people, while everybody else has made a packet out of his brilliant ideas.

LEBEDEV. Oh, for God's sake, do be quiet!

SASHA. Well, why do they talk nonsense? This is so
boring, it really is. It's Ivanov this, Ivanov that – there's
no other topic of conversation. (*Heads towards the door, and
turns back.*) I'm astonished. (*To the young people.*) Truly
astonished, that you can put up with this, ladies and
gentlemen. Don't you ever get fed up, sitting around like
this? The very air reeks of boredom! Why don't you say
something, go on? Entertain the ladies, get up off your
backsides for once! Go on, and if you've nothing to say
except about Ivanov, then sing or dance, why don't you?

LEBEDEV (*laughs*). Go to it, my girl, that's it, give 'em hell!

SASHA. No, listen to me, you owe me at least that much. If
you don't want to sing, dance, or laugh – if that's all too
boring, then please, I implore you, for just once in your
lives, out of curiosity, or novelty's sake, or just for the fun
of it, put your heads together, and think up something
witty, something dazzling – say something rude or vulgar
if you like, as long as it's funny and original. Either that,
or do some small unremarkable thing together, not
worth calling an achievement, but something to make
these ladies, just once in *their* lives, sit up and take notice!
Now, listen – I mean, you do want to please, don't you,
so why don't you try? Good God, it's all so negative, it's
all wrong, it really is. One look at you, and the very flies
drop dead, and the lamps start smoking. It's not good
enough! I've told you a thousand times, and I'll tell you
again – it's all wrong, wrong, wrong!

IVANOV *and* SHABELSKY *enter by the door at right.*

SHABELSKY. Who's this making speeches? Sasha, my dear girl, is it you? (*Laughs, and shakes his head.*) Many happy returns, my angel – may you live to be a hundred, and not be born a second time!

ZINAIDA (*delightedly*). Nikolai Alekseyevich, Count! . . .

LEBEDEV. Aha! Who's this I see? The Count! (*Goes to meet him.*)

SHABELSKY, *catching sight of* ZINAIDA *and* MRS BABAKIN, *holds out his arms to them.*

SHABELSKY. Two piggy-banks on one settee! . . . A sight for sore eyes! (*Greets them, then to* ZINAIDA.) Zinaida, my darling! (*To* MRS BABAKIN.) And my little ball of fluff!

ZINAIDA. I'm so pleased! And you, Count, we see you so rarely. (*Shouts.*) Tea, Gavrila! Now, sit down, do, please!

She stands up, goes out by the door at right, and returns almost immediately, looking extremely worried. SASHA sits down on her former seat. IVANOV greets everyone without speaking.

LEBEDEV (*to* SHABELSKY). So, where have you popped up from? What brings you here, eh? This *is* a surprise, Count, you old reprobate, where are your manners? (*Leads him by the arm downstage.*) Why do you never come and see us? You're not annoyed with us, are you?

SHABELSKY. How am I supposed to get here – ride on my walking stick? I don't have any horses of my own now, and Nikolai won't take me with him – I've got to stay and keep Sarra company, so she won't get bored. You send me your horses, and then I'll come.

LEBEDEV (*waves his hand dismissively*). Yes, well – Zina would sooner explode than send the horses. And you're my best and dearest friend. We're all that's left from the old days, you and I. Yes, how does it go? 'In you I love my years of suffering, in you I love my misspent youth . . . ' Joking aside, I feel like crying . . . (*Kisses* SHABELSKY.)

SHABELSKY. Stop, stop – let me go. You stink like a brewery.

LEBEDEV. My dear boy, you can't imagine how bored I get here, cut off from all my friends. I feel like hanging myself out of sheer . . . (*Quietly.*) With this moneylending business of hers, Zina's frightened off all the decent people, and as you can see, I'm left with the dregs – all these Dudkins and Budkins . . . Anyway, have some tea.

GAVRILA *hands* SHABELSKY *a glass of tea.*

ZINAIDA (*to* GAVRILA, *anxiously*). What on earth are you doing, you wretch? Bring some jam – gooseberry or something.

SHABELSKY (*laughs, to* IVANOV). There now, what did I tell you? We had a bet on the way over, that Zinaida would trot out the gooseberry jam the minute we arrived!

ZINAIDA. Still the joker, I see, Count. (*Sits down.*)

LEBEDEV. Yes, they've made twenty barrels of the stuff, and she doesn't know what to do with it.

SHABELSKY (*sitting down at the table*). Still coining it in, Zinaida? You must be a millionaire by now, eh?

ZINAIDA (*with a sigh*). Yes, it might look as if we're filthy rich, but where does it all come from? It's just talk, that's all.

SHABELSKY. Oh, for sure, yes – we know! We know how badly you play that hand. (*To* LEBEDEV.) Now, come on, Pavel, the truth – haven't you made your first million yet?

LEBEDEV. I've no idea. Zina deals with all that.

SHABELSKY (*to* Mrs BABAKIN). And our darling little ball of fluff will soon be a millionaire too! She gets prettier and plumper not just by the day, but by the hour! Yes, that's what it means to have pots of money.

MRS BABAKIN. I'm much obliged to you, Your Excellency, but I don't like being mocked.

SHABELSKY. My darling little piggy-bank, who's being mocked? It's simply the feelings of a full heart, rising unbidden to the lips. I love both you and Zinaida to distraction! (*Gaily.*) Ecstasy! Joy unconfined! I can't look at the pair of you and remain unmoved.

ZINAIDA. You're just the same as ever. (*To* YEGORUSHKA.) Yegorushka, put out the candles. What are you wasting them for, if you're not going to play?

YEGORUSHKA *stands up, snuffs the candle, and sits down.*

(*To* IVANOV.) Nikolai Alekseyevich, how is your wife's health?

IVANOV. Not good. The doctor confirmed just today that she has tuberculosis.

ZINAIDA. Surely not? What a shame! (*Sighs.*) And we're all
   so fond of her . . .

SHABELSKY. Nonsense! Absolute rubbish! There's no
   tuberculosis, it's more damned doctors' sharp practice, a
   confidence trick. Our distinguished medicine man's just
   looking for an excuse to hang around, so he's dreamed
   up this tuberculosis. Just as well her husband's not
   jealous.

   IVANOV *makes an impatient gesture.*

   As far as Sarra herself is concerned, I don't believe a
   thing she says or does. Doctors, lawyers, and women –
   I've never trusted them my whole life. Sheer nonsense,
   charlatanism, and conjuring tricks!

LEBEDEV (*to* SHABELSKY). You're full of surprises,
   Matvei. You put on this absurd act of misanthropy, and
   wave it around like a child with a new toy. You're no
   different from the next man, but when you start talking,
   it's as if you're choking on your own bile.

SHABELSKY. So, d'you want me to embrace rogues and
   vagabonds, or what?

LEBEDEV. Where do you see these rogues and vagabonds?

SHABELSKY. Present company excluded, of course, but –

LEBEDEV. But what? You're putting on an act.

SHABELSKY. An act, is it? Fair enough, if you've no
   principles left.

LEBEDEV. What do you mean, I've no principles? I'm
   sitting here, waiting to kick the bucket – that's my

principle. Frankly, my friend, life's too short for your
kind of philosophy. (*Calls out.*) Gavrila!

SHABELSKY. And never mind shouting for Gavrila –
you're beginning to get a nose on you like a beetroot!

LEBEDEV. Who cares, my friend? It's not my wedding day.

ZINAIDA. It's ages since Lvov's been here – he's quite
forgotten us.

SASHA. I can't abide him. Oh, he's virtuous to a fault –
can't so much as ask for a glass of water, or a light for
his cigarette, without making a show of his transparent
integrity. Walking or talking, it's practically inscribed on
his forehead: 'I am an honest man.' It makes me sick . . .

SHABELSKY. The doc? Narrow-minded and straitlaced.
(*Mimicking.*) 'Stand aside – here comes the honest man'!
He can't make a move without squawking like a parrot.
Thinks he's another Dobrolyubov. And anyone who
doesn't squawk is a scoundrel. His outlook on life is
amazingly profound. If a peasant happens to have a bit
of money, and makes a decent living, he has to be a
crook or a swindler. I wear a velvet coat, and have a
valet to dress me, so I must be a filthy tyrant. Yes, he's
as honest as the day is long, and fairly bursting with it.
He never lets up – even I'm frightened of him. Oh yes –
you get the feeling he'll punch you in the nose any
minute, or call you a crook.

IVANOV. I find him very wearing, but I quite like him.
He's so sincere.

SHABELSKY. Some sincerity. He comes up to me yesterday
evening, and right out of the blue, he says, 'I dislike you

intensely, Count.' Well, thank you most humbly! And
that's not the only thing – there's always some attitude
behind it. His voice trembles, his eyes blaze, his knees
start knocking . . . To hell with this phoney sincerity, I
say! Anyway, he obviously detests me, that's only natural,
I'm well aware of that myself, but to speak like that to
anybody, face-to-face? I'm a pretty trashy individual, but
my hair's turning grey, I mean, really! It's cheap, that's
all I can say, and heartless, this so-called honesty of his.

LEBEDEV. Well, you were young once yourself, I daresay –
you should understand.

SHABELSKY. Yes, I've been young and foolish, I've gone
after plenty of rogues and vagabonds in my day, but I've
never in my life called a thief a thief to his face, never
stooped to that level of downright bad manners. I've
been properly brought up. But this dimwitted doctor of
yours would be in seventh heaven, he'd have reached the
pinnacle of achievement, if the fates granted him the
opportunity, in the name of his humanitarian principles,
to punch me in the nose, and below the belt, in public.

LEBEDEV. Young people always have some bee in their
bonnets. An uncle of mine was a Hegelian, and he used
to fill his house with guests, get drunk, and stand up on a
chair, and declaim: 'You're all ignorant! You're the forces
of darkness! A new life is dawning!' And so on, and so
forth. Yes, he let them have it, both barrels!

SASHA. So what did the guests do?

LEBEDEV. Nothing. Just listened and got drunk. I actually
challenged him to a duel once – my own uncle.

Something to do with Sir Francis Bacon, I think. I can remember sitting there, just where Matvei is now, and my uncle and the late Gerasim Nilych were standing over there, where Nikolai is. Anyway, Gerasim Nilych asked him a question, and . . .

Enter BORKIN *through the door at right, dressed in his Sunday best, carrying a parcel, and hopping up and down, humming a tune. A cheer goes up.*

LADIES. Mikhail Mikhailovich!

LEBEDEV. Mikhail! Misha! Am I hearing right?

SHABELSKY. The life and soul of the party!

BORKIN. And here I am! (*Rushes up to* SASHA.) Noble *signorina*, may I make so bold as to congratulate the universe on having given birth to such a miraculous blossom as your good self! . . . And as a tribute to my joy, I venture to offer you . . . (*Hands her the parcel.*) A few fireworks and Bengal matches of my own making. May they light up the night, as you light up the shadowy places in this realm of darkness! (*Bows theatrically.*)

SASHA. Thank you.

LEBEDEV (*laughing, to* IVANOV). Why don't you get rid of that creature?

BORKIN (*to* LEBEDEV). Pavel Kirillych! (*To* IVANOV.) My patron! *Nicolas – voilà –* ho-hee-ho! (*Goes round all the guests.*) Most revered Zinaida Savishna . . . Most divine Marfa Yegorovna . . . Most ancient Avdotya . . . Most illustrious Count . . .

SHABELSKY (*roars with laughter*). The life and soul of the party! He's only just arrived, and the whole atmosphere's changed, have you noticed?

BORKIN. Phew, I'm worn out! I think I've said hello to everybody. So, ladies and gentlemen, what's new? Anything special, to hit us right between the eyes? (*Brightly, to* ZINAIDA.) Oh, listen, dear lady . . . (*To* GAVRILA.) Gavrila, my man, let's have some tea – and no gooseberry jam, please! (*To* ZINAIDA.) Yes, on my way over here, I spotted some peasants stripping the bark off your willow trees, down by the river. Now, why don't you turn all that over to an agent?

LEBEDEV (*to* IVANOV). Really, why don't you get rid of him? He's a crook.

ZINAIDA (*alarmed*). Well, honestly – it's never entered my mind.

BORKIN (*does some arm exercises*). I can't keep still. Now, my dear, couldn't we do something special, just for a change? Marfa, I'm on top form – I'm absolutely exalted! (*Sings.*) 'Once again I stand before thee . . . '

ZINAIDA. Yes, do something, do – before we all die of boredom.

BORKIN. Come on, ladies and gentlemen – why all the long faces? Sitting there like so many stuffed dummies! Let's play a game or something – what would you like? Forfeits, skipping ropes, hide-and-seek, dancing, fireworks?

LADIES (*clapping their hands*). Fireworks, yes, fireworks! (*They rush out into the garden.*)

SASHA (*to* IVANOV). Why are you so fed up today?

IVANOV. I've got a headache, Sasha, and I'm bored . . .

SASHA. Let's go into the drawing room.

They go out by the door at right; everybody then goes out to the garden, leaving only ZINAIDA *and* LEBEDEV.

ZINAIDA. Now, that's more like it – that young man's only been here a minute, and he's cheered us all up. (*Turns down the large lamp.*) They're all outside in the garden – there's no point in wasting candles.

LEBEDEV (*following her around*). Zina, my dear, we really ought to put out some snacks for our guests . . .

ZINAIDA. I mean, all these candles – people'll think we're made of money. (*Snuffs the candles.*)

LEBEDEV (*still following her*). Zina, listen – we'd better give them something to eat. These young people must be starving, the poor things. Zinaida –

ZINAIDA. The Count hasn't finished his tea. That's a waste of sugar. (*Goes out at door, left.*)

LEBEDEV. Ugh! (*Exits to the garden.*)

SASHA *and* IVANOV *re-enter by the door, right.*

SASHA. Everybody's gone out to the garden.

IVANOV. That's the way things are, Sasha, my dear. I used to work hard, and think a lot, and never got tired. Now I do nothing, and think about nothing, yet I feel worn out, body and soul. My conscience bothers me day and night, I feel terribly guilty, but I've no idea what I've done wrong. I mean, there's my wife's illness, money worries, the constant nagging, gossip, idle chatter, that stupid creature Borkin . . . I detest my home, it's torture having to live there. I tell you honestly, Sasha, I find my wife's company unbearable – my wife who loves me. You're a good friend, I know you won't be angry if I speak freely. Here I've come to you for a bit of enjoyment, but I'm bored even here, I feel like going back home. I'm sorry, but I'll just slip out quietly now.

SASHA. Nikolai Alekseyevich, I know what you mean. All your unhappiness stems from loneliness. What you need is someone you could love, and who would understand you. Love is the thing that would make a new man of you.

IVANOV. For goodness' sake, Sasha, a love affair? That's the last thing I need, a clapped-out old wreck like me. God preserve me from *that* sorry state! No, my clever young lady, an affair's not the answer. I say this before God – I can endure anything, the heartache, the neurosis, financial ruin, losing my wife, my own premature ageing, and loneliness – what I can't stand is despising myself. I'm ashamed even to think of it, that I'm fit and healthy, and carrying on like some village Hamlet, or Manfred, or what do they call it now? 'Superfluous man', yes. Goddammit, I could die of shame! Some pathetic individuals actually find that flattering, to be called a new Hamlet, or a superfluous man, but I think it's contemptible! It offends my pride, and makes me ashamed, it honestly pains me . . .

SASHA (*jokingly, through tears*). Nikolai Alekseyevich, let's run away to America!

IVANOV. I'm too lazy to go as far as the front door, and you're off to America . . . (*They walk over to the garden door.*) Do you honestly find it hard, Sasha – living here? You know, when I look at the people around you, I think it's frightful. Who are you going to marry in this place? Your only hope is if some young army lieutenant, or student, should happen to pass through and carry you off.

ZINAIDA *enters by the door at left, holding a pot of jam.*

Excuse me, Sasha, I'll catch you up . . .

SASHA *exits into the garden.*

Zinaida, I have a favour to ask of you . . .

ZINAIDA. Yes, Nikolai Alekseyevich, what do you want?

IVANOV (*hesitant*). Well, it's like this, you see . . . The interest on my loan falls due the day after tomorrow. You'd be doing me a great obligement, if you'd give me an extension, or allow me to add the interest on to the capital. I haven't any money at all at the moment . . .

ZINAIDA (*alarmed*). Nikolai Alekseyevich, how can this be possible? What way is this to do business? No, no, don't even think of it. Now, don't bother me with this, for God's sake, I've enough trouble.

IVANOV. I'm sorry, I'm sorry. (*Exits to the garden.*)

ZINAIDA. Ugh! Dear God, he gave me quite a turn – I'm trembling all over, absolutely shaking. (*Exits by the door at right.*)

KOSYKH *enters by the door at left, and crosses the stage.*

KOSYKH. I had diamonds, the ace, King, Queen, and seven or eight small cards, the ace of spades, and one . . . yes, one little heart, and dammit to hell, she couldn't declare a small slam! (*Exits by the door at right.*)

AVDOTYA *enters from the garden, along with* FIRST GUEST.

AVDOTYA. I could tear her apart, the tight-fisted old misery, I really could! It's not funny, I've been sitting here since five o'clock, and she's not even dished up so much as a stale herring! What a house! And what a way to run it!

FIRST GUEST. And the sheer boredom of it, it'd drive you to dash your brains out against the wall! God forgive me, but what people! I'm so bored and hungry I could bite somebody, like a ravenous wolf!

AVDOTYA. That's how I feel – I could tear her apart with my bare hands, sinner that I am.

FIRST GUEST. Well, I'm going to have a drink, old girl, then I'm off home. I don't fancy any of the young women on offer. And I mean, who gives a damn for love, when you can't even get a glass of vodka with your supper?

AVDOTYA. Let's go and find some, then.

FIRST GUEST. Sshh! Keep your voice down. There's some schnapps in the dining room, I think, on the sideboard. We'll find Yegorushka. Sshh!

They go out by the door, left. ANNA PETROVNA *and* LVOV *enter by the door, right.*

ANNA P. It's alright – they'll be pleased to see us. There's no one here, they must be in the garden.

LVOV. You know, I honestly wonder why you're brought me here, to this collection of vampires. This is no place for the likes of you and me. Decent people can't get a breath in this sort of atmosphere.

ANNA P. Now, listen to me, Mr Man of Integrity. It's not exactly good manners to take a lady out for a drive, and then keep harping on about your honesty, the whole way over. Honesty it might be, but it's a crashing bore, to say the least. You should never tell women about your virtues. Let them find out for themselves. My Nikolai, whenever he was in your situation, in female company, did nothing but sing songs and tell stories, yet everyone knew just what kind of man he was.

IVANOV. Oh, please, spare me that – don't talk to me about your Nikolai, I know his sort all too well.

ANNA P. You're a good man, but you've no understanding. Let's go into the garden. He would never say a thing like that: 'I'm an honest man! I can't breathe in this place! Vampires! Owl's nest! Crocodiles!' He left out all the menagerie, and when he did get angry now and again, all you'd hear from him would be, 'Ah well, so be it', or 'You know, Anna, I feel sorry for that man.' Just like that, whereas you . . . (*They go out.*)

AVDOTYA *and* FIRST GUEST *re-enter by the door at left.*

FIRST GUEST. There's nothing in the dining room, maybe it's in the pantry. We'll try Yegorushka – let's go through the drawing room.

AVDOTYA. I could tear her apart! (*They go out by the door, right.*)

MRS BABAKIN *and* BORKIN *enter, laughing, from the garden, followed by* SHABELSKY, *laughing and rubbing his hands.*

MRS BABAKIN. What a bore! (*Laughs loudly.*) What a bore! All walking about or sitting around like tailors' dummies. I'm so bored all my bones have started to seize up. (*Jumps up and down.*) I need to stretch my legs.

BORKIN *seizes her by the waist and kisses her on the cheek.*

SHABELSKY (*bursts out laughing and snaps his fingers*). Well, I'll be damned! (*Clears his throat.*) You know, to a certain extent . . .

MRS BABAKIN. Let me go, get your hands off me, you shameless creature – heaven only knows what the Count's thinking. Get away!

BORKIN. Angel of my soul! My heart's little carbuncle! (*Kisses her.*) Give me a loan of twenty three hundred roubles!

MRS BABAKIN. No, no, no . . . I'm sorry, but where money's involved, no thanks. No, no, no! Now get your hands off me!

SHABELSKY (*prancing around*). My little ball of fluff, what a charmer!

BORKIN (*gravely*). Anyway, enough . . . let's get down to brass tacks, put this on a business footing. Now, tell me straight, no beating about the bush, no tricks. Yes or no?

Listen . . . (*Points to* SHABELSKY.) He needs money – three thousand a year, minimum. You need a husband. Do you want to be a countess? Yes or no?

SHABELSKY (*laughs loudly*). This is amazing – what cynicism!

MRS BABAKIN (*upset*). Think what you're saying, Misha. These things just don't happen that way – all higgledy-piggledy. If the Count wants to speak for himself, then let him speak – and I don't know . . . I just . . . I mean, this is so sudden.

BORKIN. Oh, come on, don't be so coy. This is a business proposition. Yes or no?

SHABELSKY (*laughing and rubbing his hands*). Anyway, what do you say? Dammit, this is a pretty cheap trick, but why shouldn't I play it? My little ball of fluff, eh? (*Kisses* MRS BABAKIN *on the cheek.*) Delightful! Mm – tasty!

MRS BABAKIN. No, wait a minute – you've really upset me, you know. Just go away – no, don't . . .

BORKIN. Well, hurry up. Yes or no? We haven't all day.

MRS BABAKIN. I'll tell you what, Count. Come and stay at my place for two or three days. You'll have some fun there, it's not like here. Come tomorrow, do. (*To* BORKIN.) No . . . you're joking, surely?

BORKIN (*angrily*). Who's going to joke about serious stuff like this?

MRS BABAKIN. No, no, stop . . . Oh, I feel terrible! I feel absolutely awful! Countess . . . That's awful! I'm going to faint . . .

BORKIN *and* SHABELSKY, *laughing, catch hold of her by the arms and kiss her on the cheeks, as they exit by the door, right.* IVANOV *and* SASHA *run in from the garden.*

IVANOV (*clutching his head in despair*). No, it's not possible! You can't, Sasha, you can't! . . . You mustn't!

SASHA (*excitedly*). I love you madly . . . Without you, my life makes no sense – there's no happiness, no joy! You mean everything to me . . .

IVANOV. What for? What for? My God, I don't understand any of this . . . Sasha, dear Sasha, you mustn't!

SASHA. When I was little, you were my only joy – I loved you, heart and soul, as myself. And now, I love you so much. Nikolai . . . I'll follow you to the ends of the earth, I'll go anywhere you want, to the grave if need be, but for God's sake, let's make it soon, before I suffocate here . . .

IVANOV (*laughing, overjoyed*). What does this mean? Can I start all over again, from the beginning? Sasha, yes? My happiness! (*Draws her towards him.*) My youth, fresh, new life . . .

ANNA PETROVNA *enters from the garden, and catching sight of her husband and* SASHA, *stops dead in her tracks.*

IVANOV. To live? And work again?

They kiss. After the kiss, IVANOV *and* SASHA *turn round and see* ANNA PETROVNA. IVANOV *is horrified.*

Sarra!

Curtain.

ACT THREE

IVANOV's *study. A writing table, on which are scattered newspapers, books, official packages, knick-knacks and revolvers. Beside the papers stand a lamp, a carafe of vodka, a dish of herrings, some bits of bread and pickled cucumbers. On the walls hang maps, pictures, hunting rifles, pistols, sickles, whips, etc. It is midday.*

SHABELSKY *and* LEBEDEV *are sitting at either side of the writing table;* BORKIN *is sitting astride a chair in centre stage.* PYOTR *is standing by the door.*

LEBEDEV. France has a definite, clear-cut policy. The French know what they want. All they want is to bash the Huns, but it's an entirely different kettle of fish with Germany, my friend. They've got more in their sights than France.

SHABELSKY. Oh, rubbish! If you ask me, the Germans are cowards. And so are the French. They're basically bluffing each other – sabre rattling. That's as far as it'll go, believe you me. They won't fight.

BORKIN. Anyway, why should they? That's what I say. What's the point of all those armaments, congresses, all that expense? You know what I'd do? I'd round up all the dogs in the country, inject them with a good dose of rabies, and turn them loose on enemy territory. And inside a month, I'd have the enemy foaming at the mouth.

LEBEDEV (*laughs*). Well, lads, he might have a small head, but it's positively teeming with great ideas, like shoals of fish in the sea.

SHABELSKY. Sheer genius!

LEBEDEV. God bless you, Misha, you certainly keep us amused. (*Stops laughing.*) Anyway, gentlemen, it's Germany this, Germany that, but nobody's said a word about vodka. Let's have a refill! (*Pours out three glasses.*) Our good health! (*They drink and eat.*) Herring, the food of the gods! The snack *par excellence*!

SHABELSKY. Now, you can't beat cucumbers. Since the dawn of time, scholars have dreamed up nothing cleverer than pickled cucumbers. (*To* PYOTR.) Petya, be a good fellow and bring us some more cucumbers – yes, and tell the kitchen to put four onion pasties in the oven – make sure they're hot. (PYOTR *exits.*)

LEBEDEV. Caviar's also very good with vodka. Only thing is, you have to do it right . . . You take about a quarter pound of pressed caviar, two spring onions, and some olive oil. Mix it all together, and that's it – squeeze a drop of lemon on it – goddammit, the smell alone would make you dizzy!

BORKIN. Fried gudgeon goes well with vodka too – as long as you know how to cook it. You need to clean it first, then roll it in breadcrumbs and fry it until it's really crisp – crunch, crunch, crunch!

SHABELSKY. The widow Babakin gave us a nice dinner yesterday – white mushrooms.

LEBEDEV. Yes, they're very tasty.

SHABELSKY. They were done in a special way, though. You know, with onions and a bay leaf, and all kinds of spices. The minute they lifted the lid, and the steam rose up, what an aroma – absolute joy!

LEBEDEV. What do you say? Another refill, gentlemen? (*They drink.*) Our good health! (*Looks at his watch.*) Well, I can't hang about, waiting for Nikolai – I've got to go. You say you had mushrooms at the widow Babakin's? Well, I haven't seen a single mushroom here, not one. Tell me this, if you don't mind, why the devil do you keep running over to the widow Babakin's?

SHABELSKY (*nods towards* BORKIN). It's him, he wants me to marry her.

LEBEDEV. Marry her? How old are you?

SHABELSKY. Sixty-two.

LEBEDEV. Well, it's high time you *were* married. And Marfa's just right for you.

BORKIN. It's not Marfa, it's Marfa's money.

LEBEDEV. Marfa's money, is that what you're after? Fat chance.

BORKIN. Yes, well, just wait till he's married, and has his pockets filled – you'll be all over him then.

SHABELSKY. He's deadly serious, you know. This genius here is convinced I'll do what he says and marry her.

BORKIN. And what about yourself? Aren't you convinced yet?

SHABELSKY. Are you mad? When have I ever been convinced of anything? Honestly!

BORKIN. Well, thank you . . . Thank you very much! So you're going to let me down now? Yes, I'll marry – no, I won't marry – what the hell does that mean? I've already given my word of honour, you know. Are you really not going to marry her?

SHABELSKY (*shrugs his shoulders*). He's quite serious . . . an extraordinary fellow!

BORKIN (*indignant*). Well, if that's the case, why are you messing about with a respectable woman? She's desperate to be a countess, she can't eat or sleep for thinking about it, it's no laughing matter. It's dishonest, that's what it is.

SHABELSKY (*snaps his fingers*). It's actually a pretty mean trick, though, isn't it? Eh? Nasty. Well, alright, I'll give it a shot. Word of honour . . . Really, what a carry on!

Enter LVOV.

LEBEDEV. And here's our most highly respected physician. (*Extends his hand to* LVOV, *and sings.*) 'Doctor, save me, the poor man said – I'm scared to death of being dead!'

LVOV. Has Nikolai Alekseyevich come back yet?

LEBEDEV. Indeed he hasn't – I've been waiting here for half an hour.

LVOV *paces impatiently about the stage.*

So tell me, my dear Doctor, how is Anna Petrovna?

LVOV. Not good.

LEBEDEV. Shouldn't I go in and pay my respects?

LVOV. No, please don't. I think she's sleeping. (*A pause.*)

LEBEDEV. She's such a fine, sweet-natured . . . (*Sighs.*)
She was in our house on Sasha's birthday, when she
fainted . . . And I had a look at her face then, and just
knew she wasn't long for this world, poor woman. I don't
understand, though, what upset her so much. I ran in,
had a look at her – she was deathly pale, and Nikolai
was on his knees beside her – as pale as she was. Sasha
was in tears too. Sasha and I were quite upset for a
whole week afterwards.

SHABELSKY (*to LVOV*). Tell me this, revered high priest
of science – which learned man was it who first
discovered that ladies with a chest complaint respond to
frequent house calls by a young doctor? A truly
earthshaking discovery! Magnificent! And how would
you categorise it – allopathy or homoeopathy?

LVOV *is on the point of answering, but makes a gesture of
contempt, and exits.*

Hm . . . if looks could kill . . .

LEBEDEV. Why didn't you hold your tongue? What did
you want to insult him for?

SHABELSKY (*irritated*). Well, has he got to talk such
nonsense? Tuberculosis, hopeless case, going to die . . .
That's rubbish – I can't stand all that stuff.

LEBEDEV. What makes you think he's talking nonsense?

SHABELSKY (*stands up, and walks about*). I just can't accept
the idea that a normal living person should suddenly

drop dead, for no good reason. Look, let's change the subject.

KOSYKH (*runs in, out of breath*). Is Nikolai Alekseyevich in? Oh, good morning. (*Hurriedly shakes hands with everybody.*) Is he in?

BORKIN. No, he isn't.

KOSYKH (*sits down, and springs to his feet again*). Oh, well – in that case, goodbye! (*Gulps down a glass of vodka, and a morsel of food.*) I've got to go . . . Business . . . Exhausted . . . Can barely stand . . .

LEBEDEV. Where did you blow in from?

KOSYKH. From Barabanov's place. Spent the whole night playing whist, only just finished. I've been wiped out . . . That Barabanov has no idea . . . (*Tearfully.*) I mean, really – I was holding hearts all night.

Turns to address BORKIN, *who jumps back from him.*

He leads a diamond, I follow with a heart, he plays another diamond – well, I didn't take a single trick. (*To* LEBEDEV.) We're trying to make four clubs. I've got the ace, Queen, and six clubs, and the ace, ten, and three spades . . .

LEBEDEV (*covers his ears*). Enough, enough, for Christ's sake!

KOSYKH (*to* SHABELSKY). You see what I mean? The ace, Queen, and six clubs – plus the ace, ten, and three spades . . .

SHABELSKY (*pushes him away*). Go away, I don't even want to hear it.

KOSYKH. And then – disaster. The ace of spades got trounced . . .

SHABELSKY (*seizing a revolver from the table*). Go away, or I'll shoot!

KOSYKH (*waving his arms*). Dammit, you can't even talk to people now! You might as well be in Australia – no common interests, no fellow-feeling, everybody going their own way. Well, I'd better go – time I was off. (*Snatches up his cap.*) Time is money. (*Shakes hands with* LEBEDEV.) I pass!

Laughter. As KOSYKH *exits, he bumps into* AVDOTYA *in the doorway.*

AVDOTYA (*shrieks*). Dammit, you nearly knocked me down!

ALL. Aha! She pops up everywhere!

AVDOTYA. So here they are – I've been searching all over the house. Good day to you, my bold lads, I see you're being well looked after. (*Shakes their hands.*)

LEBEDEV. What are you doing here?

AVDOTYA. Business, sir. (*To* SHABELSKY.) Business that concerns you, your Excellency. (*Bows.*) I've been told to pass on best wishes, and ask after your health. And I'm to tell you, my little darling says, if you don't come over this evening, she'll cry her eyes out. That's what she says, the sweetheart – just take him aside, and whisper into his ear, on the quiet, like. But why make a secret of it? We're all friends here, it's not as if we were planning to steal the chickens, it's all legal, to do with love and mutual consent. I never touch the stuff, as God's my witness, but I'll have one to celebrate now, just for the occasion!

LEBEDEV. And I'll have one too. (*Pours out glasses.*) Yes, you're wearing well, my old trout. You've been old these past thirty years . . .

AVDOTYA. I can't keep track of the years. I've buried two husbands, and I'd marry a third, but nobody'll have me without a dowry. Eight children I've had. (*Takes a glass.*) Now then, we've made a good start, thanks be to God, and pray God we'll make a good ending. They'll have a great life, and we'll enjoy watching them. Love and best wishes to them! (*Drinks.*) That's a powerful drop of vodka!

SHABELSKY (*laughing, to* LEBEDEV). You know what? I'll tell you what's funny – they actually take me seriously, as if I'm . . . Marvellous! Amazing! (*Stands up.*) Anyway, Pavel, what d'you think? I mean, it's a pretty rotten trick, but why not, eh? The old dog on the loose again, eh?

LEBEDEV. You're talking nonsense, Count. You and I, my dear friend, ought to be six feet under – that's what we should be thinking about, not Marfa and her money. That's passed us by.

SHABELSKY. Not at all – I'm going through with it. Word of honour, I'll do it.

Enter IVANOV *and* LVOV.

LVOV. Just five minutes of your time in private, please, that's all I want.

LEBEDEV. Nikolai! (*Goes to greet* IVANOV, *and embraces him.*) Good morning, my dear friend! I've been waiting here for you a full hour.

AVDOTYA (*bows*). Good morning, sir.

IVANOV (*woefully*). Oh Lord, look at the mess you've made of my study again! I've told you all a thousand times not to do it . . . (*Goes over to the table.*) Look at this – you've spilt vodka all over my papers . . . Crumbs, pickles . . . Honestly, it's disgusting!

LEBEDEV. Sorry, Nikolai, sorry – do forgive me. We need to have a talk, my dear friend, about an extremely important matter.

BORKIN. And me too.

LVOV. Nikolai Alekseyevich, may I have a word with you?

IVANOV (*indicating* LEBEDEV). He wants to see me as well. You'll have to wait, I'm afraid . . . (*To* LEBEDEV.) What is it?

LEBEDEV. If you don't mind, gentlemen, I'd like a bit of privacy. Please . . .

SHABELSKY *and* AVDOTYA *withdraw, followed by* BORKIN *and* LVOV.

IVANOV. Listen, Pavel – you can drink as much as you like, that's your affliction, but I'm asking you please not to give my uncle drink. He never used to drink, and it's not good for him.

LEBEDEV (*alarmed*). My dear friend, I'd no idea. I didn't even give it a thought.

IVANOV. God forbid the old boy should die – it wouldn't upset you, but as for me . . . What are you doing this for? (*Pause.*)

LEBEDEV. Look, old friend . . . I don't know where to start, so this won't seem too out of place. Honestly, Nikolai, I'm so embarrassed, I feel tongue-tied, but put yourself in my shoes. I'm not my own master, I'm frankly a slave, an old dishrag . . . Please forgive me . . .

IVANOV. Forgive you what?

LEBEDEV. My wife sent me. Do me a favour, please – be my friend, and pay her that interest. Believe me, she never stops nagging me, pestering me, tormenting the life out of me . . . Get out of her clutches, for God's sake.

IVANOV. Pavel, you know I've no money right now.

LEBEDEV. I know, I know, but what d'you want me to do? She won't wait. And if she takes you to court, how can Sasha and I ever look you in the eye again?

IVANOV. I'm sorry too, Pavel, I wish the earth would open up and swallow me, but . . . but where am I to get hold of it? Just tell me – where? The only thing I can do is wait till autumn, when I can sell my crops . . .

LEBEDEV (*shouts*). But she won't wait! (*Pause.*)

IVANOV. You're in an awkward situation, pretty nasty, but mine's even worse. (*Paces up and down, thinking.*) I can't think of anything – there's nothing to sell.

LEBEDEV. Look, go and have a word with Milbakh – I mean, he does owe you sixteen hundred roubles.

IVANOV *throws up his hands in despair.*

Tell you what, Nikolai – I know you'll object, but do this old drunk a favour, for friendship's sake. Look on me as a friend . . . We were students together, you and I, young liberals . . . same ideas and interests. We both studied at Moscow University – our *alma mater* . . . (*Takes out his wallet.*) This is my secret hoard, not another soul knows about it. Take it as a loan . . . (*Takes out some money and puts it on the table.*) Swallow your pride, and look on it as a friendly gesture. I'd accept it from you, my word of honour. (*Pause.*) There it is on the table – eleven hundred roubles. You can go over and see her today, and hand it to her in person. There you are, Zinaida, you'll say – choke on that! But don't let on you got it from me, for God's sake, or old gooseberry jam-face'll kill me! (*Peers closely at* IVANOV.) Alright, then, don't. (*Quickly picks up the money, and returns it to his wallet.*) Just don't, I was only joking. For Christ's sake, I'm sorry, alright? (*Pause.*) You're depressed?

IVANOV *gestures despairingly.*

Yes, it's a business, right enough . . . (*Sighs.*) And this is just the start of your trials and tribulations. A man's like a samovar. Yes, my friend, he's not always standing cold on the shelf – now and again they shove in a live coal, and fire him up . . . Actually, the comparison's not worth a damn, but I can't think of anything cleverer. (*Sighs.*) Misfortunes strengthen the spirit. I don't feel sorry for you, Nikolai, you'll get out of this, it'll turn out for the

better, but I'm offended, and angry at people . . . I
mean, just tell me, what's the source of all this gossip?
Honestly, my friend, the kind of rumours that are flying
around, you'd expect the police to arrive any minute.
Murderer, bloodsucker, bandit . . .

IVANOV. That's all nonsense, and you're giving me a
headache.

LEBEDEV. That comes from thinking too much.

IVANOV. I don't think anything.

LEBEDEV. Well, let it all go to hell – come over to our
place. Sasha likes you, she understands and appreciates
you. She's a good, honest person, Nikolai. She certainly
doesn't take after her father, or her mother – must've
been some fine young passer-by. You know, sometimes
I look at her and I can't believe she's mine – a treasure
like that, belonging to a fat-nosed old drunk like me.
Come over and have some intelligent conversation with
her – enjoy yourself for a change. She's a loyal, sincere
girl . . . (*Pause.*)

IVANOV. Pavel – dear friend – leave me alone.

LEBEDEV. Alright, I understand. (*Hurriedly looks at his
watch.*) I understand. (*Embraces* IVANOV.) Goodbye. I've
got to attend the opening of the new school. (*Goes towards
the door and stops.*) A clever girl . . . Sasha and I were
discussing the rumours yesterday. (*Laughs.*) She came out
with a really witty remark . . . 'Daddy,' she says, 'you
know why glow-worms shine at night? It's so the birds
can see better to eat them. And that's why good people
exist, so that gossips and scandalmongers have something

to get their teeth into.' How about that, then? A genius!
Another George Sand!

IVANOV. Pavel! (*Detains him.*) What's wrong with me?

LEBEDEV. I was meaning to ask you that myself, but to be
honest, I was too embarrassed. I really don't know, my
friend. In one respect, it seems to me as if all your
various troubles were getting on top of you, but in
another, you're not the sort of person to let that happen,
I know . . . You're not easily put down. There's
something or other behind it, Nikolai, but I've no idea
what.

IVANOV. No, and I don't know either. I think . . . or else
it's . . . oh, I don't know . . . (*Pause.*) Anyway, what I was
going to say . . . I used to have a man working here –
Semyon, his name was, you remember him? One time,
when we were threshing, he was showing off to the girls
how strong he was, and he tried to hoist two sacks of rye
onto his shoulders . . . His back gave way under the
strain, and he died not long after. And now I feel as if
mine's given way. School, university, then farming,
village schools, all manner of projects . . . I believed in
different things from other people, I married differently,
got excited, took all sorts of risks, flung away my money
left and right, as you know – I've been happy, and
miserable, like nobody else in the whole country. Those
are *my* sacks of rye, Pavel . . . I've fixed them to my own
back, and my spine's cracked. At twenty we're all heroes,
there's nothing we can't do, and at thirty we're already
worn out, good for nothing. How do you explain this
exhaustion? Actually, maybe it's not so . . . No, it's not!

Anyway, Pavel, off you go, and good luck. I must be boring you.

LEBEDEV (*eagerly*). You know what? It's your surroundings, that's what's eating you up.

IVANOV. That's stupid, and it's nothing new. Go away!

LEBEDEV. Yes, it's stupid, definitely, you're right. I can see now, it's just plain silly. Anyway, I'm going . . . (*Exits.*)

IVANOV (*alone*). A pathetic, threadbare nonentity, that's me. A person would need to be equally pathetic, and worn out, like Pavel, to have any liking or respect left for me. God, how I despise myself! How profoundly I hate the sound of my voice, my footsteps, my hands, these clothes, these very thoughts. It's ridiculous, isn't it – downright morbid. Less than a year ago, I was healthy and strong, I was cheerful and tireless, energetic, working with these same hands – I could speak so even ignorant people were moved to tears. I could weep myself when I saw unhappiness, become indignant when I saw evil. I knew what inspiration was, I knew the beauty and poetry of quiet nights, when from dusk to dawn you sit at your writing table, or give way to flights of fancy. I had faith, I could look at the future, the way a child looks into its mother's eyes . . . But now, oh my God! I'm worn out, I've no faith, I spend whole days and nights doing nothing. My brain won't obey me, nor will my hands and feet. The estate's going to the dogs, the forests are groaning under the axe. (*Weeps.*) My own land looks on me as a kind of orphan. I hope for nothing, care for nothing. My heart races with fear at the very thought of tomorrow . . . And now this business with Sarra . . .

I swore undying love, held out the prospect of happiness to her, I opened up a future to her, such as she could never have dreamed of. And she believed me. For the past five years, I've watched her borne down under the weight of her sacrifices. And how exhausted she is by the struggle with her conscience, yet she's never once looked askance at me, or uttered one word of reproach. And then what? I've stopped loving her . . . How? Why? What for? I don't understand. There she is, suffering, her days are numbered, and I, like the vile coward I am, run away from her pale face, her sunken breasts, the pathetic pleading in her eyes – it's shameful, utterly shameful! (*Pause.*) My misfortunes touch the heart of a young girl, Sasha – I'm practically an old man, but she tells me she loves me. And I'm intoxicated, I forget everything – I'm enchanted, it's like music to my ears. 'A new life!' I cry, 'Happiness!' But the very next day, I believe in this new life about as much as I do in fairies. What's wrong with me? What depths have I sunk to now? What does this weakness stem from? What's the matter with my nerves? My poor wife only has to touch me on a sore spot, or a servant does something wrong, or my gun misfires, then in an instant I'm rude, and foul-tempered, not like myself at all. (*Pause.*) I don't understand it, I honestly don't – I should just put a bullet in my brain, and be done with it.

LVOV (*entering*). Nikolai Alekseyevich, I need to talk to you!

IVANOV. Doctor, if you and I are going to have an argument every day, we'll soon run out of steam.

LVOV. At least hear me out, if you don't mind.

IVANOV. I hear you out every day of my life, and I still haven't the faintest idea what you're on about. What exactly are you driving at?

LVOV. I speak very clearly and to the point, and only a man with no soul could fail to understand me.

IVANOV. The fact that my wife's at death's door – I know that, and the fact that I'm unquestionably to blame, I know that too. I also know that you're an upright, honest man, yes, I do. What more do you want?

LVOV. The sheer cruelty of people makes me so angry. A woman is dying. She has a mother and father – she loves them, and wants to see them before she dies. They know perfectly well she's going to die, and that she still loves them, but damn their cruelty – it's as if they want to make a parade of their religious zeal – they're still cursing her! And you're the man she gave up everything for – a comfortable home, her peace of mind – but you, in the most blatant manner, with the most blatant purpose, go out to the Lebedevs' house every day!

IVANOV. Look, I haven't been near the place the last fortnight . . .

LVOV (*ignoring him*). People like you need to be told straight to their faces, no beating about the bush – and if you don't want to listen, then don't! I'm accustomed to calling a spade a spade – you need this death so you can embark on some new escapade. Well, alright, but can you honestly not wait? If you allowed her to die naturally, with dignity, not grind her down with that brazen-faced cynicism of yours, would you really lose the Lebedev girl and her precious dowry? Not now, but say in a year or two, monstrous hypocrite that you are, you'd be able to turn the girl's head, and gain control of her fortune, same as now . . . So what's your hurry? Why must your wife die now, and not in a month's time, or a year?

IVANOV. This is torture. Doctor, you're not much of a physician if you think a man can restrain himself for ever. It's taking me all my strength not to answer your insults.

LVOV. Oh, come on – who do you think you're fooling? Drop the pretence.

IVANOV. Listen, Mr Clever – just think about it – according to you, I'm completely transparent – right? I married Anna so I could get my hands on a large dowry . . . They wouldn't give me the dowry, so I came a cropper on that one, and now I'm getting rid of her, in order to marry another one and grab her fortune. Right? Couldn't be simpler, absolutely straightforward. Man's such a simple, uncomplicated mechanism . . . No, Doctor, there are so many wheels and screws and valves at work in every one of us, that we simply can't judge one another on first impressions, or two or three outward signs. I don't understand you, you don't understand me – we don't even understand ourselves. You can be a first-rate doctor, and know absolutely nothing about people. Don't be so damned sure of yourself, try and see my point of view.

LVOV. Do you seriously think that you're so deep, so opaque, or that I have so little intelligence that I can't distinguish between good and evil?

IVANOV. Yes, well, you and I are never going to agree . . .
For the last time, I'm asking you – and answer me,
please, without one of your tedious sermons – exactly
what is it you want from me? What are you trying to
achieve? (*Testily.*) And tell me this, if you will – whom do
I have the honour of addressing – my wife's physician,
or my prosecutor?

LVOV. I'm her doctor, sir, and as her doctor, I demand that
you change your behaviour towards her . . . It's killing
Anna Petrovna!

IVANOV. But what can I do about that? What, tell me.
If you understand me better than I do myself, then tell
me precisely – what am I to do?

LVOV. You might at least be a bit less blatant.

IVANOV. Oh, for God's sake, listen to yourself! (*Drinks some
water.*) Leave me alone. I'm as guilty as sin, I'll have to
answer to God for that, but nobody gave you the
authority to plague me, day in, day out . . .

LVOV. And who gave you the authority to pour scorn on
my sense of right and wrong? You've tortured me,
poisoned my very soul. When I arrived in this part of
the country, I assumed there'd be stupid, crazy people,
but I wouldn't have believed there were people so
criminal as to deliberately, consciously, direct their
energies in the cause of evil. I liked people and
respected them, but now that I've seen you . . .

IVANOV. I've heard that already.

LVOV. Oh, you have, have you?

Catching sight of SASHA *approaching, wearing a riding habit.*

Well, I hope we understand each other now. (*Shrugs his shoulders and exits.*)

IVANOV (*alarmed*). Sasha, is that you?

SASHA. Yes, it's me. Good morning, weren't you expecting me? Why haven't you been to see us for so long?

IVANOV. Sasha, for heaven's sake – this is so indiscreet! Your visit could have a terrible effect on my wife.

SASHA. She won't see me – I came in by the back door. I'll be going in a minute. I've been worried – are you well? Why haven't you been to see us? It's been ages.

IVANOV. My wife's been hurt badly enough, without this. She's almost dying, and you're coming here. Sasha, Sasha, this is so silly, and cruel!

SASHA. Well, what else could I do? You haven't been to see us for two whole weeks, and you haven't answered my letters. I'm very upset. I thought you were suffering terribly here, sick, or even dying. I haven't had a decent night's sleep . . . I'll go away now, but at least tell me – are you well?

IVANOV. No, I've worn myself out, and people keep tormenting me, non-stop . . . I've no strength left. And now you're here! It's not right, it's unhealthy. Sasha, it's my fault, I'm so sorry.

SASHA. You really enjoy making these dreadful pathetic speeches, don't you. It's all your fault? Yes? You're sorry? Well, go on – tell me – what for?

IVANOV. I don't know, I don't know . . .

SASHA. That's not an answer. If you've committed some crime, you must know what it is. Forging banknotes, is that what you've done?

IVANOV. That's not funny.

SASHA. You no longer love your wife, is that it? Well, maybe so, but a person can't control their feelings, you didn't want to stop loving her. Is it your fault that she saw you, when I told I was in love with you? No, you didn't want her to see that . . .

IVANOV (*interrupting*). Et cetera, et cetera – in love, out of love, no control over my emotions. It's all so banal, so cliché-ridden. That doesn't help matters.

SASHA. You know, it's really exhausting, talking to you. (*Looks at a picture.*) That dog's very well drawn, isn't it. Was it done from life?

IVANOV. Yes, it was. And this whole affair of ours is so cheap and vulgar. He gets depressed and feels he has nothing to live for. She turns up, bright and cheerful, strong – she offers him a helping hand. It's so beautiful and convincing in a novel, but in *real* life . . .

SASHA. It's the same in real life too.

IVANOV. That shows how much you know about life! My endless whining fills you with awe, and you imagine you've found a second Hamlet, but as far as I'm concerned, that's just my neurosis, with all its accoutrements, and it's downright farcical – that's the

long and the short of it. You should have a fit laughing
at my silly antics, not sound the alarm. All this heroic
rescue stuff! Oh, I'm so angry with myself today. I feel
so wound up, as if something was ready to snap. I'll
either smash something, or . . .

SASHA. Go on, go on – that's just what you need. Break
something, smash something up, or start shouting. You're
angry with me, it was really stupid of me, coming here.
So go on, fly into a rage, shout at me, stamp your feet.
Well? Get angry, go on. (*Pause.*) Well?

IVANOV. You're funny.

SASHA. Good. I think we're smiling, don't you? Do me a
favour, if you'd be so kind – smile again, please.

IVANOV (*laughs*). You know, I've noticed – when you're
trying to rescue me, giving me all kinds of advice, you
look terribly innocent and wide-eyed, your pupils get
really huge, as if you were watching a comet. Wait, there's
some dust on your shoulder . . . (*Brushes the dust off her
shoulder.*) Yes, a naive man is a fool, but you women very
cleverly manage to be naive in such a way that you
appear sweet and wholesome, and not at all as silly as
one might think. But what is it with all of you? You're
all the same. When a man's fit and healthy, strong and
cheerful, you don't take any notice of him, but as soon
as he starts going downhill, and feeling sorry for himself,
you fling yourself round his neck. Is it honestly worse to
be the wife of a strong, bold man, than to play
nursemaid to some whining wretch?

SASHA. Much worse!

IVANOV. Why? (*Laughs loudly.*) It's just as well Darwin
doesn't know you, or he'd be after your blood! You're
ruining the human race. Thanks to you, there'll be
nothing born but milksops or neurotics!

SASHA. There's a lot men simply don't understand.
A failure is always going to be more attractive to any
woman, than a successful man, because we're all
tempted by the idea of active love. Do you understand
me? Active. Men are wrapped up in their work, and
that's why love is consigned to the background. A word
or two with the wife, a stroll in the garden, pleasantly
passing the time, shedding a tear over her grave, and
that's about it. But with us, love – well, it's our whole
being. If I love you, that means I dream about rescuing
you from your sadness, about how I'll go with you to the
ends of the earth . . . If you're on top of the world, I'm
there too – if you're in the depths of despair, so am I.
In my own case, for example, I'd be sublimely happy to
sit up all night copying your papers, or keeping watch
the whole night to see nobody disturbed you, or walk a
hundred miles on foot with you. I remember three years
ago, at threshing time, you came to us once, covered in
dust, sunburnt and exhausted, to ask for a drink. By the
time I brought you a glass of water, you were stretched
out on the settee, dead to the world. You slept about
twelve hours in our house, and I stood guard at the door,
to make sure nobody came in. And I enjoyed that so
much! The harder the task, the greater the love – that is,
the love is more strongly felt.

IVANOV. Active love . . . Hm . . . is that some sort of
perversion, or simply a woman's outlook on life?

(*Cheerfully.*) Honestly, Sasha, I'm a decent-enough man . . .
Judge for yourself – I've always loved talking, but I've
never in my life said, 'Our women are depraved,' or
'Women are headed in the wrong direction.' I've just
been grateful, that's all there is to it. Nothing more. Oh,
my dear, good little girl, you're so funny! And I, well –
I'm just a comical buffoon! Making decent people
miserable, with all this whining self-pity of mine, days on
end. (*Laughs.*) Boo-hoo, boo-hoo! (*Quickly steps back.*) But
you'd better leave, Sasha, we're forgetting ourselves . . .

SASHA. Yes, it's time I was going. Goodbye – I'm afraid
your honourable doctor may feel duty-bound to
denounce me to Anna Petrovna. Now, listen to me – go
straight in to your wife, sit down and stay with her, just
stay . . . If you have to stay a year, then so be it. If you
have to stay ten years, then do so. Do your duty. Be sorry
for her, beg her forgiveness, and weep – everything as it
should be. And above all, don't neglect your work.

IVANOV. I've got that horrible taste in my mouth again, as
if I'd swallowed a bluebottle . . . Again!

SASHA. Well, God keep you safe. You mustn't even think
about me! Just drop me a line every couple of weeks –
and thank you for that. And I'll write to you . . .

BORKIN *looks round the door.*

BORKIN. Nikolai Alekseyevich, may I come in? (*Catching
sight of* SASHA.) Oh, sorry, I didn't see you . . . (*Comes in.*)
Bonjour! (*Bows.*)

SASHA (*embarrassed*). Hello.

BORKIN. You've filled out, got even prettier.

SASHA (*to* IVANOV). So, I'll go now, Nikolai Alekseyevich.
  I'll be off. (*Exits.*)

BORKIN. A sight for sore eyes. I come for prose, and
  bump into sheer poetry! (*Sings.*) 'And you appear before
  me, like a bird to the light of day . . . '

  IVANOV *is pacing restlessly around the stage.*

  Yes, there's something about her, *Nicolas* – sets her apart
  from the rest. Isn't that so? Something special,
  something magical . . . (*Sighs.*) Actually, she's the richest
  girl for miles around, quite a catch, but her dear mama
  is such an old bat, nobody'll go near her. Everything'll
  go to Sasha when she dies, but until that happens, she'll
  give her a miserable ten thousand, some curling tongs
  and a flat iron – and for that you'll have to go down on
  bended knees. (*Rummages in his pockets.*) Fancy a smoke?
  Cigars . . . *De los majores* . . . d'you want one? (*Offers his
  cigar case.*) They're not bad . . . a decent smoke.

IVANOV (*goes up to* BORKIN, *panting with rage*). Get out of
  this house! Never set foot in this house again! Get out!
  Now!

  BORKIN *rises slightly, and drops his cigar.*

  Go – this instant!

BORKIN. What's all this about, *Nicolas*? What are you so
  angry about?

IVANOV. What? So where did you get those cigars from?
  D'you think I don't know where you take the old man
  every day, and what you're after?

BORKIN (*shrugs*). What's it to you?

IVANOV. You despicable wretch! Your plotting and
scheming over the whole county have dragged my name
through the mud. We've got nothing in common, and I'd
like you to get out of my house, this instant. (*Pacing
quickly up and down.*)

BORKIN. You're only saying that because you're in a foul
temper, I can see that, and I don't hold it against you.
You can abuse me as much as you like . . . (*Picks up his
cigar.*) But you really ought to snap out of it, you're not a
teenager . . .

IVANOV. What have I told you? (*Trembling.*) Are you trying
to make a fool of me?

Enter ANNA PETROVNA.

BORKIN. Well, Anna Petrovna's here now, I'll be off.
(*Exits.*)

ANNA P (*after a pause*). What was she doing here today?
(*Pause.*) I'm asking you – what was she doing here?

IVANOV. Anna, don't ask . . . (*Pause.*) I'm truly sorry.
Whatever punishment you want to give me, I'll bear it,
only . . . Don't ask me, please. I haven't the strength.

ANNA P (*angrily*). What was she doing here? (*Pause.*) So this
is what you're like? Now I understand. I can see at last
what kind of man you are. Despicable, beneath
contempt . . . You came and told me a pack of lies,
d'you remember? And I believed you, left my mother
and father, gave up my religion, and came to you. You

lied about truth, about goodness, and your own honourable intentions, and I believed it, every word . . .

IVANOV. Anna, I've never lied to you.

ANNA P. I've lived with you for five years. I've grown tired and ill, but I've loved you, never left you for even a single moment . . . You've been my idol . . . And then what? You've been deceiving me the whole time, in the most blatant manner.

IVANOV. Anna, don't say that, it's not true. I've made mistakes, yes, but I've never lied, not once in my life. That's something you can't reproach me with . . .

ANNA P. I see it all now. You married me, thinking my parents would forgive me, and settle money on me . . . That's what you thought . . .

IVANOV. My God – this is trying my patience! (*Weeps.*)

ANNA P. Shut up! The minute you realised there was no money, you started a new game . . . I remember it all now, and I see right through it. (*Weeps.*) You've never loved me, and never been faithful . . . Never!

IVANOV. That's a lie, Sarra! Say what you like, but don't insult me with a lie . . .

ANNA P. Dishonest, wretched man! You owe money to Lebedev, and now you're trying to worm your way out of it by turning his daughter's head – deceiving her, the same as you deceived me. Isn't that the truth?

IVANOV (*choking*). For God's sake, shut up! Or I won't be responsible . . . I'm choking with rage, and I might . . . I might say something awful . . .

ANNA P. You've always been deceiving me, quite shamelessly, and not only me. You've been pretending all these swindles and shady deals were Borkin's handiwork, but I know now whose they were . . .

IVANOV. Sarra, shut up and go away, or I'll say something really dreadful, something vile. Shut up, you Jewish bitch!

ANNA P. I won't shut up! You've deceived me for too long, I won't shut up!

IVANOV. So you won't shut up? (*Wrestling with himself.*) For God's sake!

ANNA P. Go on, go – go and deceive the Lebedev girl!

IVANOV. Then you might as well know – you're going to die soon. The doctor told me, you're going to die soon . . .

ANNA P (*sits down, in a sinking voice*). When did he say that?

IVANOV (*clasping his head in his hands*). I'm sorry. Oh, my God, I'm sorry! (*Sobs.*)

Curtain.

ACT FOUR

Between Act Three and Act Four a period of a year has elapsed.

One of the guestrooms in the Lebedev house. In the foreground, an arch, separating the guestroom from the ballroom, and doors to right and left. Antique bronzes, family portraits. Festive decorations. An upright piano, with a violin on it, and a cello standing nearby. Throughout the whole act, GUESTS move around in the ballroom, in evening dress.

LVOV (*enters, looks at his watch*). It's after four. They ought to be starting the benediction now . . . They'll bless the bride and take her to the church. There we are – a triumph for virtue and truth! He couldn't get his hands on Sarra's money so he tormented her into her grave, and now he's found another one. He'll play the hypocrite with this one too, until he's got her money, and then he'll ship her off to the same place as he sent poor Sarra. Same old story, naked greed . . . (*Pause.*) He's in seventh heaven now, ecstatic – he'll live like a king to a ripe old age and die with a clear conscience. Well, I'll burst your bubble, sir! I'll tear off that mask of yours, and everybody'll know just what sort of creature you are – I'll flush you out of your seventh heaven, and drop you into a pit so deep the devil himself couldn't drag you out of it. I'm an honest man, it's my business to step in, and make the blind see. I'll do my duty and tomorrow I'll get the hell out of this accursed place! (*After some thought.*) But what should I do? I can't talk to the Lebedevs, that's a

waste of time. Challenge him to a duel? Make a scene?
My God, I'm a bag of nerves, I'm like a schoolgirl. I
can't even think straight. What should I do? A duel?

KOSYKH (*enters gleefully, to* LVOV). Yesterday I declared a
small slam in clubs, and got a grand slam. But that
Barabanov dropped me in the mire again. We start
playing. I call one no trumps, he passes. Two clubs, he
passes. I call two diamonds . . . three clubs . . . And you
wouldn't believe it, it's quite incredible – I declare a
slam, and he doesn't show his ace. If that pig had shown
his ace, I'd have declared a grand slam in no trumps . . .

LVOV. I'm sorry, I don't play cards, so I'm afraid I can't
share your triumph. Are they going to have the
benediction soon?

KOSYKH. It should be, yes. They're trying to talk some
sense into Zinaida – she's bawling her head off, at
having to hand over the dowry.

LVOV. Not her daughter?

KOSYKH. The dowry. It's tough on her. Once he's
married, he won't pay what he owes her – you can't very
well sue your own son-in-law.

MRS BABAKIN, *like a ship in full sail, crosses the stage past*
LVOV *and* KOSYKH, *who sniggers behind his hand. She
turns and stares at him.*

MRS BABAKIN. Stupid creature!

KOSYKH *prods her waist with his finger, and bursts out
laughing.*

Peasant! (*Exits.*)

KOSYKH (*guffaws*). Woman's off her head! She was a decent-enough dish till she clapped her eyes on a title, and now you can't get near her. (*Mimicking.*) Peasant!

LVOV. Listen, tell me honestly – what's your opinion of Ivanov?

KOSYKH. A hopeless case. Plays cards like a shoemaker. Last year, at Easter, I'll give you an example – we sit down to play – me, the Count, Borkin, and him. I've got the deal . . .

LVOV (*interrupting him*). Is he a good man?

KOSYKH. Who? Ivanov? He's a slippery customer. Comes up smelling of roses, no matter what. Him and the Count make a right pair – always got an eye on the main chance. Came a cropper with that Jewess of his, though – landed in the mire, and now he's after Zinaida's moneybags. I'll bet you anything, and I'll be damned if I'm not right – he'll get rid of old Zina within a year. He'll do for Zina, and the Count'll do for the Babakin woman. They'll pocket all that lovely money, and live like lords off the fat of the land. Anyway, Doctor, you're looking distinctly whey-faced today – what's the matter? You look awful.

LVOV. It's alright, I'm fine. Had too much to drink yesterday.

LEBEDEV (*entering with* SASHA). We can talk here. (*To* LVOV *and* KOSYKH.) Right, gentlemen, clear out and join the ladies in the ballroom. We want to have a private talk.

KOSYKH (*as he passes* SASHA, *triumphantly snaps his fingers*).
Sight for sore eyes! Queen of trumps!

LEBEDEV. Clear off, caveman – just go!

LVOV *and* KOSYKH *go out.*

Sit down, Sasha my dear, do . . . (*She sits down and looks
round the room.*) Now, listen carefully, this is a serious
matter. The fact is, your mother has asked me to convey
a message to you – you understand? I don't want you to
think this is any of my doing, but your mother has told
me to.

SASHA. Daddy, get to the point.

LEBEDEV. Well, you're supposed to receive a dowry of
fifteen thousand roubles, silver. So there you are, and
there's to be no argument about it later. Now, stop –
don't say a word! This is just for starters, there's more
to come. You're supposed to receive fifteen thousand
roubles, but bearing in mind that Nikolai Alekseyevich
already owes your mother nine thousand, I'm afraid
that's to be deducted from your dowry. Now then, apart
from that . . .

SASHA. Why are you telling me this?

LEBEDEV. Because your mother told me to!

SASHA. Oh, leave me in peace! If you had the slightest
respect for me, or yourself, you just wouldn't speak to me
in that fashion. I don't want your dowry! I didn't ask for
it, and I'm not going to . . .

LEBEDEV. What are you flying off the handle at me for?
You know, Gogol's two rats had a sniff of each other

and then backed off, but you, emancipated woman and all that, don't bother to sniff, you just wade right in.

SASHA. Leave me alone, then, don't insult my ears with your vulgar calculations.

LEBEDEV (*flaring up*). Dear God, you'll have me slitting my wrists, the lot of you, or stabbing somebody! One's at it, day in, day out, shouting and bawling, non-stop nagging, counting every damn miserable kopeck – the other one's so smart, so damn humane and liberated, she can't even understand her own father! I'm insulting her ears, she says. Dammit, before I came out here to insult your ears, I was being carved up into little pieces in there! (*Points to the doors.*) And she can't understand! They've got my head splitting, I don't know whether I'm coming or going . . . Damn the lot of you! (*Goes towards the door and stops.*) I don't like this, you know. I don't like any of this.

SASHA. What don't you like?

LEBEDEV. Any of it, I don't like any of this at all.

SASHA. Meaning what?

LEBEDEV. Well, I'm not going to sit here and drone on about it. I don't like any of it, I've told you, and I don't even want to look at this wedding of yours. (*Approaches SASHA, tenderly.*) Forgive me, Sasha dearest – it may be this wedding is entirely sensible, all above board and highly principled, but there's something not right about it. It's not like other weddings. You're young, fresh and innocent, pure as the driven snow, you're a beautiful girl – but he's a scruffy-looking widower, well past his prime. And I can't make him out, God help him. (*Kisses SASHA.*)

I'm sorry, Sasha, but there's something not very nice about him. People are talking about him already – about the way his wife Sarra died, and then suddenly, for some reason or other, he's desperate to marry you. Anyway, I'm just an old woman – that's what I've become, a silly old mother hen. Don't listen to me – don't listen to anybody except yourself.

SASHA. Oh, Daddy, I feel myself there's something not right, seriously not right. Oh, if you only knew, how hard this is for me. It's unbearable. I don't feel comfortable at all, and I'm afraid to admit it. Daddy, dearest, say something to cheer me up, for God's sake – teach me what to do.

LEBEDEV. Teach you how? What?

SASHA. It's terrible, I've never known anything like it. (*Looks round the room.*) I don't think I understand him, and I never will. The whole time I've been engaged to him, he's never once smiled, never once looked me straight in the eye. It's all endless complaining, remorse for some guilt or other he keeps hinting at, trembling – I'm absolutely exhausted. At times I even feel as if . . . as if . . . well, as if I don't love him as much as I should. And when he comes over to see me, or talk to me, I get so bored. What does all this mean, Daddy? I'm so frightened.

LEBEDEV. My dear darling, my beloved only child, listen to your old father. Break it off with him!

SASHA (*alarmed*). What? What are you saying?

LEBEDEV. I mean it, Sasha. Oh, there'll be a scandal, it'll start all the tongues wagging, you'll be the talk of the whole county, but honestly, it's better to put up with the scandal, than to torture yourself the rest of your life.

SASHA. Don't say that, Daddy, don't say that! I don't even want to hear it, I've got to fight off these gloomy thoughts. He's a decent, unhappy, misunderstood man, I *will* love him, I'll appreciate him, put him back on his feet. I'll do my duty. My mind's made up.

LEBEDEV. That's not duty, that's nonsense.

SASHA. That's enough. I'm sorry I complained to you, about something I didn't even want to admit to myself. Don't tell anybody, please. Let's just forget it.

LEBEDEV. I don't understand any of this. Either I'm going senile, or you've all suddenly become very clever, but I'm hanged if I understand a thing.

SHABELSKY (*entering*). The hell with everybody, myself included! This is infuriating!

LEBEDEV. What's up with you?

SHABELSKY. No, I'm serious – I need to do something, I don't care what, something to make everybody else, not just me, absolutely disgusted. And I'll do it, my word of honour! I've already told Borkin I'm going to get engaged today. (*Laughs.*) It's all rotten, so I'll be rotten too.

LEBEDEV. Oh, I'm sick of you. Listen, Matvei, if you carry on talking like this, well, I'm sorry to say, you'll wind up getting carted off to the madhouse.

SHABELSKY. Madhouse, this house, that house – what's the difference? Do me a favour then, and take me there, I don't care. Rotten, empty-headed, useless people, and I'm sick of myself too, I don't believe a word I say.

LEBEDEV. You know what, my friend? Stuff an old sock in your mouth, set fire to it, and blow it out at people. Or better still, pick up your hat and go home. This is a wedding, everybody's enjoying themselves, and you're sitting squawking like an old crow. To tell you the truth . . .

SHABELSKY *leans over the piano, and starts sobbing.*

Heavens above! Matvei! Count! What's the matter with you? Ye gods, Matvei, dearest friend . . . I've hurt your feelings. I'm sorry, I'm a silly old goat . . . I'm drunk, I'm so sorry. Have some water . . .

SHABELSKY. I don't want any. (*Lifts up his head.*)

LEBEDEV. What are you crying for?

SHABELSKY. It's nothing, it's alright . . .

LEBEDEV. Now, Matvei, don't tell lies. What's wrong? What caused that?

SHABELSKY. I just happen to see that cello, and suddenly remembered . . . remembered that poor Jewish woman . . .

LEBEDEV. Phew! This is no time for memories. God bless her, and may she rest in peace, but this isn't the time to remember her.

SHABELSKY. We used to play duets together. A wonderful, superb woman! (SASHA *begins to sob.*)

LEBEDEV. You as well? Don't, please. Good God, they're both howling, and I . . . I . . . look, go away somewhere, the guests'll see you.

SHABELSKY. Pavel, as long as the sun's shining, you could be happy in a graveyard. And as long as there's hope, even old age isn't so bad. But I've no hope at all, none whatsoever.

LEBEDEV. Yes, you really are in a sorry state – no children, no money, nothing to occupy you . . . Anyway, what can you do? (*To* SASHA.) And what's up with you?

SHABELSKY. Pavel, lend me some money. We can settle up in the next life. I want to go to Paris, see my wife's grave. I've given away a lot in my life, half of everything I had. So I have the right to ask for a small fraction of that. And I'm asking you as a friend, what's more.

LEBEDEV (*bewildered*). My dear fellow, I haven't a bean. Oh, alright, that's fine. I can't promise, you understand, but, well, that's fine, excellent. (*Aside.*) They're really killing me.

MRS BABAKIN (*enters*). Where's my brave gentleman? Count, how dare you leave me all on my own! Disgraceful!

She raps SHABELSKY *on his arm with her fan.*

SHABELSKY (*disgusted*). Leave me in peace, I can't stand you.

MRS BABAKIN (*stupefied*). Eh? What?

SHABELSKY. Clear off, go on!

MRS BABAKIN (*slumps into an armchair*). Ah! (*Weeps.*)

ZINAIDA (*enters, weeping*). Someone's just come in – I think it's the best man. It's time for the benediction . . .

SASHA (*pleading*). Mummy!

LEBEDEV. Now they're all wailing! A quartet! For God's sake, turn off the taps! Matvei! Marfa! Honestly, you'll have me in tears next . . . (*Starts weeping.*) Oh, dear Lord!

ZINAIDA. If you've no time for your own mother, and you're not going to obey, well, just do what you like and I'll give you my blessing . . .

Enter IVANOV, *in a frock coat and wearing gloves.*

LEBEDEV. This is all we need now! What's going on?

SASHA. What are you doing in here?

IVANOV. I'm sorry, but I'd like to have a word with Sasha in private.

LEBEDEV. That's not right. You're not supposed to see the bride before the wedding. It's time you were at the church.

IVANOV. Pavel, please . . .

LEBEDEV *shrugs his shoulders. He and* ZINAIDA, SHABELSKY *and* MRS BABAKIN *go out.*

SASHA (*coldly*). What do you want?

IVANOV. I'm in a foul temper, but I can speak calmly. Listen . . . I was getting dressed just now for the ceremony, and happened to look in the mirror . . . and at the grey hair at my temples . . . Sasha, this is all wrong! It's not too late yet, we need to put a stop to this whole insane farce. You're still young, and innocent – you have your whole life ahead of you, and I . . .

SASHA. That's nothing new, I've heard it a thousand times, and I'm fed up with it. Go on ahead to the church, you can't keep people waiting.

IVANOV. I'm going home right now, and you can tell your family there'll be no wedding. Tell them anything. It's time we came to our senses. I've been playing Hamlet, and you've been the starry-eyed *ingénue*, but it's all over.

SASHA (*flaring up*). What way is that to speak? I won't listen.

IVANOV. Well, I'm speaking, and I'll go on speaking.

SASHA. What have you come here for? These complaints of yours are beginning to sound like mockery.

IVANOV. I'm not complaining now. Mockery, you call it? Yes, I'm mocking. And if I could mock myself a thousand times harder, and set the whole world laughing, I'd do it, believe me! I caught sight of myself in a mirror, and it was as if something inside of me just snapped. I started laughing at myself and nearly went mad with shame. (*Laughs.*) Melancholia! Noble grief! The sublime mystery of misery! All that's lacking now is for me to write poetry. Moaning and groaning, inflicting my pain on other people, knowing that my energy's sapped and gone for ever, that I've run to seed, that I've outlived my usefulness, become feeble-minded, sunk up to my neck in these nauseating fits of depression – to feel this way in bright sunshine, when even an ant is content to carry its

burden – no, thank you very much. To realise that some
people think you're a charlatan, and some take pity on
you – others hold out a helping hand, while a fourth
lot – they're the worst of all – they listen to your sighs,
awestruck, see you as some great prophet, a second
Mohammed, and wait for you to present them with
some new religion! No, thank God I still have some
pride and conscience. I was laughing at myself on the
way over here, and I felt as if the very birds and even
the trees were laughing at me.

SASHA. This isn't anger – this is lunacy.

IVANOV. You think so? No, I'm not mad. I'm seeing things
in a different light now, and my thoughts are as clear
and pure as your own conscience. We love each other,
but there'll be no wedding for us. I can rant and rave as
much as I want, but I've no right to destroy other
people. I poisoned my wife's last year of life with my
whining. Since we've been engaged, you've lost the
ability to laugh, and grown five years older. Thanks to
me, your father, who used to have a pretty clear outlook
on life, no longer understands people. When I go to a
meeting, or visit friends, or go hunting, I carry my
boredom, gloom and depression everywhere with me.
No, don't interrupt – I'm being brutally direct, I'm
choking with rage, I'm sorry, but this is the only way
I can speak. I never used to lie, never complained about
life, but once I'd started grumbling, against my will,
without even noticing, I found fault with everything,
cursing my fate, moaning non-stop, so that anyone
listening to me becomes infected with the same revulsion
towards life, and starts complaining too. And what an

attitude – as if I was doing nature a favour by living! Yes, damn me to hell!

SASHA. Stop. What you've just said makes it clear that your depression is eating you up, and it's time to begin a new life. And that's a good thing . . .

IVANOV. I don't see anything good about it. And what sort of new life is there? I'm completely done for, beyond any doubt. It's time we both understood that. New life, indeed!

SASHA. Oh, Nikolai, don't be silly. Who says you're done for? What's all this cynicism? No, I don't want to talk, or listen – go on ahead to the church!

IVANOV. I'm done for!

SASHA. Stop shouting, people can hear!

IVANOV. If an intelligent, well-educated, healthy man suddenly becomes thoroughly miserable, without any obvious reason, and starts rolling down the slippery slope, he'll keep on rolling, and there'll be no stopping him – there's no salvation for him. Where was my salvation? What is it? I can't drink – wine gives me a headache. Write bad poetry? I wouldn't know how. Should I pray to my own mental inertia, and see it as something worth exalting? I can't. Inertia is just that – inertia. Weakness is weakness – I can't call them by any other name. I'm done for, totally finished – there's nothing more to say. (*Looks round the room.*) We might be interrupted. Listen, if you love me, help me. Break it off with me, immediately, this very instant. Hurry.

SASHA. Oh, Nikolai, if only you knew how you've worn me out. How you've tortured my very soul. You're a kind, intelligent man – judge for yourself: how can you ask anyone to do such a thing? Each day you set some new task, harder than the day before. I wanted an active love, but this is martyrdom!

IVANOV. And if you were to become my wife, the tasks would be even more impossible. Break it off, now. Listen to me – it's not love that's speaking to you, but your own stubborn integrity! You've set yourself the goal of saving me at all costs, of resurrecting the man in me, and you've flattered yourself that you could perform that feat. Now you're ready to give up, but you're being held back by false emotion. Can't you see?

SASHA. What strange, wild logic! Anyway, how can I break it off with you? How can I reject you? You've no mother, no sister, no friend. You're ruined, your estate's being broken up, people talk about you behind your back.

IVANOV. It was stupid of me to come here. I should've done what I intended . . .

LEBEDEV *enters.*

SASHA (*runs to meet* LEBEDEV). Daddy, for God's sake – he's run in here like a mad thing, and he's torturing me! He's demanding I break the wedding off, he doesn't want to ruin me. Tell him I don't want his generosity, I know what I'm doing.

LEBEDEV. I've no idea what you're talking about. What generosity?

IVANOV. The wedding's off.

SASHA. No, it's on. Daddy, tell him the wedding's going on.

LEBEDEV. Wait, wait, hold on! Why don't you want a wedding now?

IVANOV. I've told her why, but she doesn't want to understand me.

LEBEDEV. No, never mind telling her, tell me, so I'll understand. Ah, Nikolai Alekseyevich! As God be your judge – you've caused so much upset in our life, that I feel as if I'm living in a chamber of horrors. I see nothing, and understand nothing . . . It's like a punishment. Well, what do you suggest I do – an old man like me? Challenge you to a duel?

IVANOV. There's no need for that. All you need is to keep your head, and understand plain language.

SASHA (*pacing agitatedly round the stage*). This is terrible, terrible! He's like a child!

LEBEDEV. There's nothing left but to throw up your hands. Listen, Nikolai – no doubt you think this is all very clever and subtle, and in accordance with the laws of psychology. But to me, it's a scandal, and a disaster. Now, hear me out – listen to an old man, one last time. This is what I'm saying to you – relax, take it easy, the way everyone else does. Everything in life's simple – the ceiling is white, boots are black, sugar is sweet. You love Sasha, she loves you. If you love her, stay – if you don't love her, go. We won't make any fuss. So you see, it's quite simple. You're both healthy, intelligent, decent people – you're well fed, thank God, and clothed . . . what else do you want? You've no money? Is that so hugely important?

Money won't bring happiness. Of course, I can understand
. . . you've mortgaged your estate, you can't pay the
interest. But I'm a father, I understand . . . Her mother
can do what she likes, and good luck to her – if she
won't give you any money, then never mind. Sasha says
she doesn't need a dowry. These principles of hers, it's
like Schopenhauer, it's all nonsense. I've got ten
thousand roubles tucked away in the bank . . . (*Looks
round.*) Not a soul in the house knows about it – your
grandmother's money – it's for the two of you. Take it,
only you've got to give Matvei a couple of thousand . . .

The GUESTS *are assembling in the ballroom.*

IVANOV. Pavel, there's no point in discussing this – I'm
going to do as my conscience bids me.

SASHA. And I'm going to do as *my* conscience bids *me*. You
can say what you like, I'm not calling off the wedding.
I'm going to fetch Mummy now. (*Exits.*)

LEBEDEV. I don't understand this at all.

IVANOV. Listen, old man . . . I'm not going to try and
explain to you whether I'm good or bad, sane or neurotic.
I was young once, ardent, sincere, intelligent – I loved,
and hated, and believed, differently from other people.
I worked hard enough, and hoped hard enough, for ten
people. I tilted at windmills, banged my head against
brick walls. Without measuring my own strength, with
no judgement or knowledge of life, I heaved a load onto
my back, instantly tearing my muscles and crushing my
spine. I was in a fearful hurry to sow my wild oats, I
drank too much, got too excited, worked too hard, did

nothing by halves. But tell me – what else could I have done? I mean, there's so few of us, and so much work, so very much. And look how cruelly life takes its revenge on me, how hard I've had to struggle with it. I simply cracked under the strain. At the age of thirty, permanently hungover, like an old man, shuffling around in his dressing gown. My head's bowed, I'm slow on the uptake, exhausted, shattered, broken-winded – I've no faith, no love, no aim in life, I'm like a spectre, drifting through the crowd, without knowing who I am, what I'm living for, or what I want. Love is all nonsense, it seems to me, affection's mere affectation, there's no sense in work, songs and rousing speeches are cheap and out of date. I drag my misery around with me wherever I go, my cold indifference, displeasure, disgust with life. I'm absolutely finished! Before you stands a man, already worn out at thirty, disenchanted, crushed by his own worthless achievements – he's burning with shame, jeering at his own weakness. Oh, how my pride rebels, I'm choking with fury! (*Staggers.*) God, how am I going to get away – I can hardly stand – I'm so weak. Where's Matvei? Tell him to take me home . . .

VOICES (*in the ballroom*). He's here! The best man's here!

SHABELSKY (*entering*). In a rusty frock coat, somebody's cast-off, and no gloves, of course. That's why I'm getting all these funny looks, stupid jokes and idiotic grins. Loathsome creatures!

Enter BORKIN, *hurriedly, carrying a bouquet and wearing a frock coat, with a best man's buttonhole.*

BORKIN. Whew! Where on earth is he? (*To* IVANOV.)

They've been waiting ages for you at the church, and you're here, making speeches. It's actually funny. Dear God, it's hilarious! Anyway, you can't go along with the bride – you'll have to go separately with me, and I'll come back from the church and fetch her. Do you honestly not understand me? This is ridiculous!

LVOV (*enters, to* IVANOV). What, are you here? (*Loudly.*) Wait, Nikolai Alekseyevich – I want everyone to hear this! You're a scoundrel, sir!

IVANOV (*coldly*). I thank you most humbly. (*General uproar.*)

BORKIN (*to* LVOV). That's a gross insult, sir – I'm challenging you to a duel!

LVOV. Mr Borkin, I consider it degrading even to talk to you, let alone fight. Nikolai Alekseyevich can seek satisfaction or whatever, as his own conscience dictates.

SHABELSKY. I'll fight with you, sir.

SASHA (*enters, to* LVOV). What for? What are you insulting him for? Gentlemen, please, let him tell me.

LVOV. Miss Lebedev, I didn't insult him for no reason. I've come here as an honest man, to open your eyes, and I beg you to hear me out.

SASHA. What can you say? That you're only being honest? You'd do better to examine your own conscience, and tell me if you actually know what you're doing! You come in here, a shining example of integrity, and fling the most terrible insults at him, which almost kills me. Before that, you were following him around, like a shadow, making his life a misery, utterly convinced you were just doing your duty as a man of honour. You got mixed up in his private life, blackened his good name, and set yourself up as his judge. Whenever you could, you bombarded me and all his acquaintances with anonymous letters – all the while imagining you were only being honest. You thought it was the honourable thing to do, you didn't even spare his sick wife, you gave her no peace with your suspicions. Frankly, there's no rotten trick, no cruel piece of chicanery, you didn't get up to, yet you fancy yourself to be an extraordinarily honest and progressive man!

IVANOV (*laughs*). This isn't a wedding, it's a debating hall! Hear, hear!

SASHA (*to* LVOV). Now, you think about that – do you know what you're doing, or not? Stupid, heartless people! (*Takes* IVANOV *by the hand.*) Come on, Nikolai, let's go! Daddy, let's go . . .

IVANOV. Go where? Wait, I'll put a stop to all this! The young man in me's waking up at last, it's the old Nikolai who's speaking now! (*Pulls out a revolver.*)

SASHA (*screams*). I know what he's going to do – Nikolai, for God's sake!

IVANOV. I've been rolling downhill too long now to stop. It's time I was on my way. Get back! Thank you, Sasha!

SASHA (*shouts*). Nikolai! For God's sake! Stop him!

IVANOV. Leave me alone! (*Runs to the side and shoots himself.*)

Curtain.

Pronunciation Guide

Where the stress in English polysyllables tends to fall on the penultimate syllable, Russian stress patterns are much less predictable, and this can give rise to difficulty. The following is a rough guide only to the correct pronunciation of names which occur in the dialogue.

Alekseyevich	Ah-lek-SAY-yeh-vitch
Avdotya	Ahv-DAW-tyah
Babakin	Bah-bah-KEEN
Balabalkin	Bah-lah-BAHL-keen
Barabanov	Bah-rah-BAH-noff
Borkin	BAWR-keen
Dobrolyubov	Daw-braw-LYOO-boff
Gavrila	Gahv-REE-lah
Gerasim	Geh-RAH-seem
Ivanov	Ee-VAH-noff
Korolkov	Kaw-rawl-KOFF
Kosykh	Koh-SEEKH
Lebedev	LAY-bed-yeff
Lvov	LVAWFF
Matvei	Mat-VAY
Mikhail	Mee-KHAYL
Mikhailovich	Mee-KHAIL-oh-vitch
Misha	MEE-shah

Mushkino	Moosh-kee-NO
Nikolai	Nee-koh-LIE
Nilych	NEE-litch
Ovsyanov	Awv-SYAH-noff
Pavel	PAH-vel
Petrovna	Peh-TRAWV-nah
Petya	PEH-tyah
Plesniki	Pleh-snee-KEE
Pyotr	PYAWTR
Sarra	SAH-rah
Shabelsky	Shah-BYELL-ski
Yegorovna	Yeh-GOH-rov-nah
Yegorushka	Yeh-GOH-roosh-kah
Zarevsky	Zahr-YEHV-ski
Zinaida	Zee-nah-EE-dah
Zaimishche	Zah-EE-meesh-chay